Acknowledgme

- To my very talented wife Linda, who continues to provide inspiration, astute feedback, and encouragement.

- To my children Shale, Jacqueline, and Sabrina, whose insights are as unique as they are.

- To the students at the Schulich School of Business, who thought they were learning from me, but in reality gave me a chance to become a student again. And to Joseph Palumbo, Minoo Bhutani, Alyson Gampel, and the rest of the excellent staff at the Schulich Career Development Centre, from whom I have also learned tremendously.

- To the staff of the Canadian Institute of Chartered Accountants, and particularly Karen Duggan and John Tabone, for their feedback and support.

- To my team of reviewers, who provided invaluable feedback on many early drafts, including John Craig, Larry Goldberg, Brian Grosman, Jean-Marc Hachey, Wallace Immen, Jordan Kalpin, Sylvia Link, John R. V. Palmer, Michael Sasarman, Mary-Coleen Shanahan, and Julia Woods.

- To David Maister, who has left an indelible mark on the world of professional services, and whose ideas inspired some of my own.

- To my many clients over the years who asked for my help with their business challenges. And to those same ones who asked for my advice with their career planning.

- To my long-time collaborators, Despina Zanganas and Sandra Shaul.

- To Shannon Skinner, who has unfailingly helped to amplify my message to a wider audience.

- To Peter Harris and Melanie Douglas at Monster.ca, for also helping me get my message out.

- To Mark Haak and David Johnson of Swerve Design Group, and my editor, Wendy Thomas.

ACKNOWLEDGMENTS

- To Mikey, because I still don't know what he does for a living.

- To my many former colleagues, too many to mention here, who helped me to mature as a manager. To my coaching clients, who challenged me with their unique situations and who sought my counsel. And to my friends, who accept my counsel, whether asked for or not.

- To those who have led interesting careers and have shared them with me: Christina Elder, David Goorevitch, Burt Konzak, Amir Raubvogel, Sandy Salem, Carol Seidman, Bruce Winstanley, and Cheryl Zeldin. And to the dozens of others who also left a bit of themselves on the pages that follow, by sharing their stories and advice.

PERSONAL BALANCE SHEET

Foreword

I have known Randall Craig for only three years, but his impact on my life has been remarkable. Originally hired as a consultant for my organization, he established himself as a trusted partner and a true professional. Randall is a person of depth, with both impressive academic credentials and meaningful client engagements to his credit. He is a talented career coach, a visionary leader, and an inspiring change agent. Whether he is delivering a keynote or running a workshop, he commands attention and reflects energy back to the audience.

As the leader of the Career Development Centre of the Schulich School of Business, I have met thousands of professionals who are looking to understand how they can add more meaning, make a difference, or obtain more "success" in their lives. Most haven't yet mastered the important life skill of career planning; in fact, most don't even know where to start.

We live in a *free agent* era where we have more options, more flexibility, and more say. Yet with this new-found flexibility comes responsibility. How can we strategically make better choices along the way? How can we reduce risk, yet get a better return on our career investment? In this book, Randall provides the practical frameworks, processes, and tools for career planning – but not before helping us obtain a clear focus for our professional lives.

He asks the tough questions like *What will be your legacy?* or *How do you define success?* – questions far more important than the mechanics of resumé writing, interviewing, or even networking. Answering his questions helps ensure that our role is one where we can make a difference, obtain better work-life balance, and achieve greater career satisfaction.

Gone are the days when we can rely on our manager, HR department, mentors, or recruiters to manage our careers. And likewise, our families provide important support, but they aren't career planning experts either. All of these groups can provide input, but when all of it is collected, how should it be organized? How to balance *what we like* with *what we want*?

I have met hundreds of people who have been touched by Randall Craig's brand of career planning. Now his thoughtful perspective and common-sense frameworks are available in a definitive, practical how-to guide. Like those hundreds of others, no matter how much success you may have achieved so far, this book can provide you an even tighter focus – and a more efficient route to your goals.

If you are in Human Resources or accountable for attracting, retaining, and developing talent in your organization, think of this book as a practical supplement to your current policies and a great empowerment tool for your employees. At the same time, let's all agree on where career planning responsibility should rest: as HR professionals we can help, as organizations we can provide the opportunities (and the support). But each individual employee must take responsibility for his or her own career. The same applies to work-life balance.

If we expect our employees to be responsible, then we should also provide them the career planning tools to make it happen. Recently, I reread Randall Craig's first career planning book and realized that he was talking to me. I am now using his frameworks and information to guide my own career development plan. What will my next step be? Stay tuned – but for the first time in many years, I feel that I have clarity concerning both my personal and professional goals. As you go through this book, I expect that you too will develop clarity – and the motivation to achieve your goals.

Joseph Palumbo
Executive Director, Career Development Centre
Schulich School of Business, York University
Toronto, Canada
May 2007

Introduction

Forty years, 10,000 days, 80,000 hours. Measure it any way you like, but this is about how much time you spend on the job throughout your career. With so much of your life spent working, does it not make sense to also spend time planning it in an organized, strategic manner?

Enter Career Planning, one of the most important skills you will learn:

- Career planning ensures that you are spending those 80,000 hours in a fulfilling, challenging, enjoyable way.

- Given your significant investment in your training and your valuable business experience, career planning ensures that you find the highest and best use for your time: a career return on investment.

Yet career planning cannot occur in a vacuum. How you spend your time beyond the working day can have a direct impact on your success within it. As a simple example, the positive support (and input) from a life partner can make your transit considerably easier.

This book was named the *Personal Balance Sheet: A Practical Career Planning Guide* on purpose: choosing a-balance-for-you helps define your priorities. Managing your career provides for the balance you have chosen.

This book is designed to demystify and provide practical, step-by-step guidance on the process of career planning. Throughout it, you will find a number of diagnostic exercises that help you understand your strengths, and frame your career development and work-life balance plans. And more importantly, you will pick up practical ideas that can help you translate your plan into action.

Finally, the book recognizes that your employer[1] has an important supporting role to play. They provide an infrastructure for your professional growth and a support group of managers, HR professionals, mentors, and colleagues. By following this book's frameworks, you will learn a vocabulary that will make it easier to discuss ideas with your managers and gain their support. The Personal Balance Sheet is designed to supplement existing HR processes – not replace them.

An important point to make is that career *planning* is not synonymous with career *change*. While people do make changes throughout their careers, many don't. These people – and you may be one – seek to develop a deeper, broader, stronger understanding within their area of expertise. Wherever your career takes you, and whatever type of balance you desire, what you do is yours to choose. **This book gives you the tools to develop your plan, and the motivation to achieve them.**

The book is divided into six sections, each designed to move you along your path. Depending on how much career-related thinking you have already done, your entry point may not be at the beginning of this book. If this is the case with you, consider scanning from the beginning anyway; many of the initial concepts are referred to later.

1. **Career planning fundamentals:** Learn about career planning basics. Chapters in this section also cover the workplace, the general business environment, and introduce three assessment models.

2. **Work-life balance:** Do you work to live, or live to work? This section introduces the Personal Balance Sheet as a model for determining the type of balance that is right for you.

3. **Developing your career:** This section explores the many possible career paths, and describes how to collect the experience necessary to be successful.

---

1 Throughout this book, the terms *employer, organization, company,* or *firm* all refer to your workplace and can be used interchangeably. The actual type of organization could be a corporation, partnership, not-for-profit, regulator, or any other kind of entity. The term *manager* refers to the role of the person you report to. Their real title could be anything: President, Director General, Partner, Executive Director, CFO, Senior Manager, Manager, etc.

4. **Looking at the options:** How do you set your career goals? Using the models introduced earlier, learn to develop a tighter career focus – and understand the mechanics of change.

5. **Achieving your goals:** At this point, your focus needs to change from knowledge to action. This section reviews all of the necessary "action" skills, from networking, to job search skills, to strategies for talking to your manager. It introduces the Career Commitment Chart and the concept of Filling in the Gaps.

6. **Long term success:** Finally, how do you maintain your success throughout your career? This section reviews business development skills, how to adjust to change, and using an extended leave.

Since no one knows you better than yourself, there is no one better equipped than you to determine your goals and how to achieve them.

Career Planning Fundamentals

Chapter 1:
What Have You Achieved?

CHAPTER IN A FLASH: *Frameworks within this book (Personal Balance Sheet, Reality Check Interviews, etc.) help give you the confidence to make career decisions. The earlier you start career planning, the better.*

No matter where you are in your career, there is no doubt that you have achieved some degree of success. You went to an excellent university or college. You took courses, which for the most part provided intellectual challenge. Along the way you made lifelong friends – and maybe even met your significant other. You asked people for advice: your parents, friends, professors, and countless others. And because of this, you made an important decision: you knew what you wanted to "be" in life!

While you may not have recognized it at the time, you were engaged in the process of career planning, the subject of this book. Because life was simpler back then, you didn't need to worry about your family obligations. You didn't need to worry about mortgage payments, client deadlines, social appearances, or other pressures. Since the whole world was full of opportunity – and it still is, really – the choices you made seemed to have far lower risk.

The payoff has been your technical, functional, and industry experience. Over the last five-ten-plus years, your exposure to many issues has given you a confidence that you didn't have at the very start of your career. The flip-side is that you have become so good at your day job, tasks that you rarely do – like career planning – are often seen as risky or low priority and are thus avoided. Yet as responsible professionals, we're certainly capable: if we understood the career planning process, then we would more likely engage in it.

Benefits of Career Planning

Regrettably, career planning doesn't guarantee a quick route to promotion. It means choosing for yourself how you want your career to progress, within the context of an appropriate-for-you work-life balance. Despite the fact that you may have the same title as others, and you may be doing the same job as others, your particular career and work-life balance requirements are exclusively yours.

How can a book on career planning possibly tell you the answer? If you look at other book categories – diet books stand out – they have no such problem telling you precisely what you must do. They say that if only you follow their system to the letter (eat only grapefruits, for example), you will successfully lose weight. For those few people who really do enjoy eating grapefruit, this is not a problem; for everyone else the advice is impractical. Said another way, how can a career planning book possibly avoid this very trap?

This book is very different. In it, you will find a number of frameworks (the *Personal Balance Sheet*, *Job Quality Checklist*, *Reality Check Interviews*, etc.) that are not prescriptive. That is, *your* responses to each framework will help you determine *your* next steps. And since each person will respond uniquely, your next steps will also be uniquely your own.

Visualize Your Future

Imagine yourself, perhaps a few years beyond retirement. Or better yet, enjoying a well-deserved early retirement. What do you see? You're on the beach enjoying a life of luxury. Your children and grandchildren come to visit you and comment on how fit you are. Thankfully, you have enough money salted away that you can live comfortably. You spend your days exploring your surroundings and your evenings as president of your condominium corporation.

While this might not be your exact picture, consider it for a few minutes. How did this outcome come to be? How is it that you are healthy, while so many others are troubled with issues? When did you have grandchildren? How did you become so financially well-off? And where did you get those skills to become a community leader?

Maybe it was luck? Not likely.

Career planning is all about providing you with the concepts and tools so that "luck" has very little to do with it. Once you understand these concepts, you can use them throughout your career to chart your own course to that future.

Why Now?

There is an old Chinese proverb that asks the question "When is the best time to plant a tree?" The answer, of course, is 20 years ago. The proverb continues: "When is the second-best time to plant a tree?" The answer is *right now*. The earlier that you are able to start career planning for yourself, the more likely you will achieve your goals. If you haven't started to do so yet, not to worry: the second-best time to start is when? Right now!

It's much easier to plan your career when you're at the top of your game.

This is fundamentally the opposite approach to the "if it ain't broke, don't fix it" school of thought. If your career (or something at home) suddenly "breaks," you will be under extreme stress. You may not be able to make rational choices, your options may be limited, and there may be little time to fill in the gaps. It is precisely at the time when you are achieving the most success that you should be considering your career path. Banks know this too: it's much easier to get a loan when you don't need one, than when you do.

Decision-making 101

When you go to purchase a new suit, how do you make the decision? How do you commit to actually making the purchase? Sometimes, logic leads the way: you notice your comfortable (but thread-bare) old suit is starting to wear out and decide to go to the store to make a purchase. While you are there, you use your emotions to help decide on the color and style. Other times, emotion leads the way: you see a suit that looks wonderful, and then you rationalize on why you "need" that particular suit, right now.

The suit purchase is a fairly low-risk purchase. Making changes to your career (or proposing marriage, or buying your first house) is much, much riskier. You might be offered a new role, but unless there is congruency between your feelings on the subject and your logical analysis of it, often there is little movement. Difficulty in making decisions has nothing to do with laziness – it has everything to do with having enough data to allow your decision to be made without second-guessing, and without regret.

Said another way: if you can't rationalize your emotional decision, it is not likely that you will make a decision. Within this book are more than a dozen frameworks designed to provide you with the analytical data points that underpin your analysis; these will spur you to action – and career success.

At the same time, those same people you asked for advice before you started in the working world (parents, friends, etc.) have now been supplemented with people at your workplace: managers, colleagues, HR professionals, mentors, and others. Speaking to this new group can provide perspective and support – and another boost to your career confidence.

Goal-setting

You may have had some experience with strategic planning in your professional life. You set the goal and then engage in tactics to achieve that goal. These tactics may be in the areas of marketing, accounting/finance, operations, or HR. When it comes to strategic planning at an individual level, however, this model begins to fall apart. What if we don't have a defined career goal? We certainly don't have a marketing department, nor any other department. We don't have a board of directors, and we don't have people we can delegate responsibilities to. But we may have spouses, kids, older parents, friends, a boss, client responsibilities, and other "things" that get in the way. (Later, in Chapter 5, you will go through a process called Reality Check Interviews, that will help you productively focus your goals.)

The purpose of career planning is to generate movement towards a goal

For this reason, the purpose of career planning isn't to achieve a goal, but to start movement toward it, to generate momentum. As we make progress, we learn more about where our "real" goal might be and subtly change our direction – and the things we do each day. Where we end up is a function of doing the right things along the way, both at work and in life. Said another way, the journey is the destination – and we will end up at precisely the destination we deserve.

Infrastructure

As a reminder, it is inappropriate to work on your own "account" during the day. While your employer will benefit from your personal investment and self-development efforts (aka Filling in the Gaps, Chapter 14), unless they specifically allow on-the-job time for these activities, use your own time – don't steal theirs. And also don't take their supplies, use their Internet bandwidth, borrow their computers, or do your personal work on their premises. If you don't already have a home office, Appendix Two provides a good starting point for what you'll need.

FOCUS

- A career plan is the roadmap for achieving your career goals.
- The frameworks in this book provide objective data points that will help you make better career-related decisions.
- The best time to start is NOW!

Chapter 2:
What Problem Are You Trying to Solve?

CHAPTER IN A FLASH: *To do career planning requires time: this chapter provides specific suggestions on how to find it. One of the challenges of modern life is the expectation of speed, both at home and on the job. To progress in your career, you must work within the constraints of this velocity and, for any problems that appear, solve them at their roots.*

We spend more time at work, or thinking about work, than pretty much any other activity in life. So when things don't go exactly the way we expect, we sometimes become disenchanted and think about quitting. The essence of career planning is that we should be running to our next challenge, and not running *from* something we don't like. So defining the problem is usually the first step in solving it.

Is there really a problem?

You may believe that the "problem" is related to determining the next step in your career: after all, this is a book on career planning. But it is important to recognize, and possibly rule out, other factors that may be obscuring the picture. For some people, these factors are distractions, which should rightfully be ignored, while for others, these factors are exactly what must be addressed. Unless they are, they may continue to masquerade as a problem with the job – now, and in the future.

Let's look at some of the typical problem areas that prevent us from taking the time to think about and plan our careers.

Life Velocity – Find the Time

If you speak to retirees about your typical day, they are amazed at how much is going on. They are glad to be away from the rat race; they don't know how you do it.

Let's look at the modern rat race a bit more closely. After some degree of success you likely have a house or condo of your own, a car or two, a membership at a health club (and possibly also a golf club). If you have children, they may go to a private school, but whether they do or not, they are certainly involved in extracurricular activities: dance, music lessons, soccer, swimming, or tennis. If you live in a major city, your commute to work takes at least an hour of your day – if you're not on a road trip meeting prospective clients. Your mortgage and other financial commitments are almost overwhelming; your time obligations surely are. And all of this on top of your job responsibilities.

You think to yourself, "How did I get myself into this situation?" Like the retirees, you say to yourself, "I'm so busy, I don't know how I do it!" But do it you must, because if you stop, you worry about not being able to start up again. There just isn't enough time in the day!

Despite all these competing pressures, there are many ways to mitigate the problem of life velocity. If you are really serious about managing your career, time is needed for both reflection and planning. And there are a number of important, but time-consuming activities that need to be done. Time is also needed to read this book! To manufacture some time, you either need to change your current priorities, become more productive, or cut things from your schedule. Here are a few suggestions that might help:

Time is needed both for reflection, and planning.

- **BUILD EXERCISE INTO YOUR ROUTINE.** Not only will this reduce your general stress level, but you will look better and feel better, and your body will last longer. Even though exercise takes time away from your day, you will return to work more alert and more productive.

- **TAKE A 24-HOUR VACATION EACH WEEK.** Remember the concept of a day of rest? Why not institutionalize it in your life? Recharge your batteries by not working, not shopping, not answering your cell phone, and not using your computer one day each week.

- **SCHEDULE "FOCUS TIME."** Give yourself permission to take some time each day specifically for thinking and reflection. Personally, I do my best thinking when I'm exercising. Not consciously thinking, but letting my brain work on a problem in the background. For you, it may be some other way, but it is certain that your best "thinking" time is not when you have phones ringing, emails chiming, or deadlines imminently looming. Unless we are able to cordon off time each day specifically for thinking and reflection, it is unlikely that we will actually think or reflect.

- **GO TO A DAY SPA.** It's surprising what some concentrated pampering can do to your state of mind.

- **TAKE YOUR VACATIONS!** Think about your vacation entitlements: do you take all the vacation that you earn? If you don't take at least three weeks off each year, over time, you'll probably burn yourself out. I always planned my vacations in places where I can't be reached: touring rural China, for example. Even local travel can give you a whole new perspective.

- **TAKE AN EXTENDED VACATION OR SABBATICAL.** University professors have known about the rejuvenating impact of a short-term change of pace for many years. Why can't you do the same? Consider how taking a month (or three) off can improve your perspective.

Later in this book, we'll look more thoroughly at the issue of achieving balance and the connection to career choice. For now, the objective is simply to capture enough time to reflect and plan.

Family Problems

How often do you come home from a tough day at work and "take it out" on your family? Or clam up, and don't do or say anything until it's too late? When you have a great day, it shows, and everyone is happy with the collective good fortune. If you have an awful day and blow up, everyone (including yourself) feels bad. We oscillate between these two behaviors, although not always to the extremes.

And what if your home life is not positive or supportive? What is the impact when you go into work after a big fight, or with news that your children are failing in school, or with news that a parent has just been diagnosed with a terrible disease? There is *always* an impact.

Your family can be the foundation of your support network – if you let them be.

We might take it out on our co-workers. Or maybe we smother ourselves in our work and pretend that no problems exist at home (and thereby aggravate the very problem that our attention requires). When times are bad, we need to look to our family and friends for support, but we sometimes find it difficult because we are so out of practice.

No matter how much we might try, dissatisfaction (or satisfaction) at home will affect the job and vice versa. No matter how you look at it – glass half-full or glass half-empty – you shouldn't divorce the family because of the job, nor quit the job because of a problem in the family. Solve the problem at its root, or it will surely repeat itself on the next go-round.

On the flip side, a relationship that allows for involvement in the career-planning process builds a strong foundation for good times and bad. Risk can be shared, along with success. The positive role that a life partner plays can be as much a factor in your success as the relationship you have with your managers, peers, and staff.

Job Velocity

A friend, top of his class in engineering and one of the brightest lights in his Ivy League law class, decided to interview at major New York law firms for one of the coveted first-year technology law positions. As was done in this type of situation, he was interviewed by about a dozen partners and associates during the day, one after the other. The office was beautiful, it had a busy excitement that was equally alluring, and the pay was lucrative.

He was shown into the first interviewer's office; the interviewer described working life and painted a picture of a firm that "works hard and plays hard." The next person he met was also very positive on the organization, as was the third, who noted that the firm brought in a catered dinner when a team was working late on a deal.

My friend noticed that behind each office door there was a thin futon standing upright; he decided to ask what it was for. The answer? If you have to work through the night, the futon can be used to sleep on, so as to minimize transit time. The next person told him that a fresh shirt is purchased for each person after an all-nighter. And the final interviewer that day described the great breakfasts that are catered after all-nighters.

How tied are you to your job, both during the day, and after?

The postscript: He could have had the prestige and financial rewards of a top New York firm, but at what cost? After hearing from his boastful would-be colleagues how great the firm was, he decided that this wasn't the place for him. Instead, he has had an excellent career at a top-notch firm in California, living, working, and raising a family there for the last 20 years.

Consider what has happened to the velocity of business over this time period. At one time, faxes were sent only for urgent materials; there was no email, nor voicemail; senior executives often used "secretaries" for both dictation and personal errands. Today, it is not uncommon for some managers to receive 50 to 75 (and more) emails per day, as well as dozens of voicemails. And when we are out of the office, we have these systems programmed to auto-reply or forward to our cell phones. Some people put only their cell phone number on their business cards and then don't turn the cell phones off at the end of the day. In some organizations, the use of instant messaging, screen sharing, and BlackBerries are creating whole new ways to be accessible – and interrupted.

There are some advantages to this huge increase in velocity: improved client service, better risk management, and better resource utilization. And

No matter how hard we try, there can only be 24 hours in each day.

at the individual level, many of us thrive under the pressure – it makes us better at what we do.

The pressure of speed is not a problem in and of itself – but the problem is who or what is in control. If you don't control the velocity, it will control you. Here are some simple ideas, once again provided to help you find time for planning and reflection:

- Set firm time boundaries. For example, resolve not to work after 10 p.m. or before 7 a.m.

- Consider, for example, your increased productivity (and your reduced stress) if you limited email access to two to three times per day, rather than "instant response."

- Just as you likely do with paper that crosses your desk, prioritize tasks that come in through these new channels (e.g., voicemail, email, mobile text messaging, instant messaging) and deal with them according to your priorities and timing.

- Consider forwarding your cell phone to voicemail both during meetings and when you require uninterrupted time to think. Turn your cell phone off at night.

- Consider again the impact if you took 15 minutes each morning, before you started your workday, just for yourself. This *focus time* could be used to help set your daily priorities both in the context of your job and your career planning activities.

- Think about taking 15 minutes after your workday, both to recap what you learned during the day, and then disengage from it.

Notwithstanding these suggestions, it's important to understand how job velocity has suddenly crept up on you. Do you (or others) believe that you are irreplaceable in your job? Are you catching up on your work only at night and over each weekend?

As an executive at an international public company, I would talk to our clients about the benefits of being a global organization and our ability to work on problems 24 hours each day. For example, if an issue came up in North America, it could be solved by the folks overseas while North America slept. I and others would describe the benefits of throwing the work "over the fence" at the end of our business day and arrive the next morning to see the problem solved, in our email boxes.

The reality, though, was a bit different. At about midnight, the email traffic from the early risers in the U.K. would start. By 2 a.m., the rest of

Europe and the Middle East would add their traffic. To ensure that the problem got solved, you would respond to the emails as they came in. Meanwhile, others would see that you were on-line, as you all use the same instant messenger program. You open a chat window to discuss the issues in real time. But typing is inconvenient, and the language gap makes communications this way cumbersome; before long, you're on the phone. Emails are still streaming in, though, and others are opening chat windows to you, asking "quick" questions. And you're still on the phone. All this at 2 a.m.

In this situation, the increased velocity was caused by the promise to the client. Recall who made that promise about "throwing the work over the fence"?

There is no question that certain times of the year (quarter-ends, busy season, etc.) will force your priorities, but presumably there is a quid pro quo: when it isn't busy, you can take some time for yourself.

No Balance

All of these issues, and similar ones, fall under the category of not having balance and perhaps not feeling like we are in control over our lives. Some of the issues take place at the office, and some of them take place at home. Conveniently, we are told by our managers, our friends, and our families that we need to solve the problem by "getting balance," as if balance were a product sold on store shelves.

As you may recognize, achieving your appropriate balance and choosing how to manage your career are both examples of gaining control over your life. For many, the stress is caused merely by not having a plan to follow or benchmarks for comparison. This book is named the *Personal Balance Sheet: A Practical Career Planning Guide* for a good reason: choosing a-balance-for-you helps define your priorities. Managing your career provides for the balance you have chosen. Said another way: we work to live, we don't (or rather shouldn't) live to work.

The person who knows you best is the one who can best define your balance. That person is you.

The solution to the problem of *no balance* can't be found in workshops on time or stress management. Nor can it be found at your workplace. Since only you can choose the type of balance you would like, only you can solve this problem. This book suggests a practical approach to doing this – and how to plan your career along the way.

FOCUS

- Life is full of challenges: some are at home, some are at work, and some are on the sports field. Recognize these challenges for what they are, then consider how you can address them.

- Don't quit your job because of a problem in the family; likewise, don't lose your family because of a problem at the job.

- To successfully develop your career, you need time to think and reflect. Give yourself permission to take some time, each day, to do this.

- We are in control of our lives only when we have control over both our work-life balance and our career.

- Life is not a dress rehearsal: make every minute count.

Chapter 3:
Taking Stock of the Workplace

CHAPTER IN A FLASH: *Career planning is not about planning change – it is about planning your career. Since you likely work with others at an organization, anything that you do is influenced by this context: organizational process, support systems, teamwork, industry leadership, multiple career paths, job security, name recognition, bureaucracy, and the 20-70-10 rule. Each of the people you interact with can teach you something important about career planning and work-life balance as well: the Political Wolves, Image Managers, One-Dimensional Wonders, Stupid Ones, and Hoarders.*

What we make of ourselves is most strongly related to our experience on the job. Because of the amount of time we spend at work, our colleagues start as role models, and many become our friends. We leave work happy when we do a great job, and we leave unhappy when things don't go as planned.

Our workplace provides both emotional and professional support; this helps us mature into successful managers. By taking stock of the work environment, you will have the contextual knowledge required for career planning. Be sensitive to the judgments you make as you read on: what you see as a negative may be someone else's key success factor: some people thrive in a highly structured organization, for example, while others find it too restrictive.

1. Organizational Process and People Knowledge

As you move up the organizational ladder, your internal network and knowledge grow exponentially. Your credibility with your managers, peers, and subordinates lets you get things done more easily than others, and you always know whom to call when there is a problem that needs solving.

While this is positive for you as an individual, organizations are now seeing the other side: with lowered employee loyalty, specialized knowledge is also an area of business risk. What if the only person who understands a certain process leaves? Or if Jennifer, the only one who understands the history of client X, gets hired by a competitor?

Firms reduce this risk by cross-training and by rotating client teams. From a personal perspective, this is a huge benefit: your personal value increases with each new experience you collect.

One of the more interesting trends today is that of *Knowledge Management* (KM). We certainly like the idea of being called *knowledge workers*, and as leaders, the idea of managing a *learning organization* is flattering. KM seeks to extract organizational knowledge, automate it, and make it available to anyone within the organization, when they need it. The promise of each of us working up to our potential, with the lubricating comfort of others' knowledge, is satisfying.

But what if you have become an expert exclusively in internal processes? You know how to fudge "the system" to get things done. You know whom to call within the organization for help. And you know the client histories and relationships intimately.

A former colleague found herself in this type of situation but was able to use it completely to her advantage. She worked at one of the largest financial institutions in the country, and it was her knowledge of its internal systems that allowed her to earn a series of promotions. After a number of years she was looking to make a change by moving outside her institution, but was concerned that too much of her value was tied up in her internal "system" knowledge and personal relationships.

She realized that she would have to limit her job search to companies that valued her system knowledge and internal relationships as highly as her business acumen. In the end, she found a senior-level position working at a supplier to her former employer: her old department became her client. She turned a definite weakness into something that clearly differentiated her from other candidates. And while the nature of the relationship changed, her network remained the same.

2. Tremendous Support Systems

Most mature managers will attribute their success to their team: their subordinates, peers, and managers. We rely on these people to make decisions on our behalf, exercise judgment, and point out when our decisions don't make sense. Their success often means our success. And when we work with them for many years, the collective team begins to develop a strong bond, both personally and professionally.

Support departments await our beck and call. Computer doesn't work? Call IT. Questions about a payroll change? Call HR. Reports to copy, bind, and then deliver? Call the Mailroom. Need some giveaways for a new client meeting? Call Marketing. Each of these areas (and others like them) is staffed with specialized and trained people. Each area has preferential deals with a host of suppliers.

We also receive support from our mentors. How often have they steered us through difficult decisions? Or put in a good word for us when it really counted? The value of your mentor is their organizational knowledge coupled with their interest in you. When you make a change – any change – be prepared for the nature of the mentoring relationship to change as well.

Large organizations are fully functioning entities, organized in a self-supporting web of relationships, support departments, and systems. If you leave, be prepared to relearn where these support systems can be found. If you follow an entrepreneurial path, be prepared to personally learn how these support systems work as you undertake each time-consuming task yourself. Your employer has helped you become more efficient in your day job and has allowed you to develop the focus necessary for a successful career. If you stay, you will continue to benefit from this.

The longer you stay with an organization, the stronger your built-in support system.

3. Teamwork

A larger organization provides a significant number of opportunities to work in a team environment, whether it be on a client service team, standing committees, or special projects. You work with different people, learn new technical skills, and get exposed to new business issues. And when your teammates aren't perfect, it's not a problem: the project, or the engagement, will eventually end.

Probably the biggest benefit to teamwork is hidden. Over the years, you develop a vast network of individuals throughout the organization who can support you and whom you can trust. Beyond the connections you make with those in your workgroups, there is often a strong culture of giving throughout the entire organization.

Earlier in my career, I was leading an engagement to help a local company connect with foreign suppliers. Anyone I called within the global organization gave me a few minutes of their time, no matter how busy they were. And I did the same whenever someone called me. This culture of giving – Give to Get – is the basis of developing relationships internally. *It is also the basis of developing business – and relationships – externally.*

Many people who leave an organization are disappointed at losing both the network and this strong culture of giving, especially as this has been partly responsible for their success so far. Maintaining connection, both through informal contacts and formal alumni programs, can help.

4. Industry Involvement and Public Leadership

Larger organizations will invest in industry and public leadership for several reasons:

- They are big enough to afford it.
- They feel that there is an obligation to contribute back to their industry.
- Their economic and marketing interests are served.

At an individual level, that means there may be more opportunities for personal growth: speaking at conferences, advising regulatory bodies, setting industry standards, etc. Involvement in leadership also provides direct connection to other leaders, as they will also be participating in the same conferences and regulatory bodies as you.

5. Multiple Career Path Options

"Up or out" is the mantra at some larger firms. And at smaller companies, promotion is very difficult because of longer staff retention, fewer boxes on the organizational chart, and the problem of successful succession. For different reasons, direct promotion may not be possible in both types of organizations. As the size of the organization increases, there would be a number of other appealing paths that can stem from any one position.

Assume that you are an accountant now at the manager level. Your next move might be to the senior manager level. But it could also be to a number of other worthwhile positions:

- Manager for a more strategic client.
- A move to a specialized group, such as Valuations, Tax, or Forensic Accounting.
- A secondment to a special project.
- A staff role in marketing, HR, IT, etc.

Each of these positions, although possibly lateral moves, would give you special skills that would ultimately position you for an even more senior role, either internally or externally. Large organizations give you several internal options for promotion; small companies might provide only one.

6. Job Security

We like to think that working in a larger organization provides a degree of job security that smaller organizations just cannot provide. Insolvency is usually not a daily worry, nor is meeting payroll. If you are a more senior manager, you are often the person making the decisions, not just being affected by them.

The reality, however, is that company size doesn't matter. Job security is a function of the current economic health of your employer and your fit with them.

And even if you are let go, pretty much every firm recognizes the value of alumni: keep them happy, and the alumnus will provide referrals for years.

7. Name Recognition

When you are interviewing candidates for a position, are you more or less likely to give consideration to someone who comes from a recognized brand name? You think to yourself, if they could make it at IBM, then they could make it at your company. Otherwise (you think to yourself) they would have been fired long ago.

The brand equity of a recognized company rubs off on its employees, effectively guaranteeing that they meet a minimum standard of quality. Your employer's name gives you some bragging rights – you've made the cut, and others haven't.

Titles do a similar thing. Does a person have what it takes to sit in the corner office? You think to yourself: if they did it before, they can do it again. And in your own case, there usually is some degree of satisfaction when looking at your own business card with the title VP, Partner, or President.

8. Bureaucracy and Process

Process is a very good thing: it instills fairness and order and helps institutionalize accountability. The problems start, however, when there is so little empowerment in the bureaucracy that the rules become an end in themselves. Rather than common sense, policies and procedures often get in the way of meeting customers' and other stakeholders' needs: the rules become more important than achieving objectives.

I recall working with a major financial institution several years ago. A manager was describing to me the internal policies and procedures that governed their working days. The policies were printed out and put in binders for easy reference. These binders filled two shelving units, eight feet wide. Today, of course, intranets have greatly reduced the need for policy binders and storage shelves, but the policies and procedures still exist, hidden within intranet sites. While some of the regulations were probably government mandated, and others were internal audit requirements, I just couldn't believe the sheer volume of them. No wonder so many large institutions have poor reputations for customer service. Who could possibly remember all the policies and procedures, let alone the reasons for them!

Process and bureacracy may be similar, but are not the same.

On the other hand, process ensures that training takes place, that people are considered for possible promotion, and that knowledge is maintained within the organization. Another factor: different types of individuals thrive in different types of environments. Those who enjoy structure often find that it permits focus on their personal objectives.

9. Two 20-70-10 mantras

One of Jack Welch's famous management mantras is the 20-70-10 rule. The top 20% of the people in an organization are stars. The bottom 10% are the dogs, and the remaining 70% are those who are stuck in the middle, partially disengaged. The challenge in management is to recognize and promote the top 20, engage the middle 70, and fire the bottom 10. If these three things don't happen in your organization, there will be a slide to the mediocre. If you are in the middle 70, your key reason for career planning is to help you become engaged.

It probably is worthwhile contrasting Jack Welch's 20-70-10 with a different 20-70-10. In this second model, the top 20% are those whose focus is clearly on advancement. The bottom 10% hate their jobs and probably should move on. The middle 70% generally enjoy what they do, perform decently, and whose balance choices are fairly broad. If you feel you are in the wrong group, your key reason for career planning is to help you find the right one.

10. Personalities

One of the greatest benefits of working is the social connection you make with so many people. Consider the following types of people, and ask yourself whether you are starting to take on their characteristics: the Political Wolves, Image Managers, One-Dimensional Wonders, Stupid Ones, and Hoarders. Each one has an edge, but each also holds a lesson for either career planning or work-life balance.

POLITICAL WOLVES: Political Wolves often are more concerned about achieving a personal objective than a group one. When a request comes their way, how do they think?

"Okay, let's do it!" or

• "Why is he asking?"

• "What's in it for me?"

• "I'll say yes, and then do nothing, just to get him off my back."

• "Can I screw him? Last time he didn't help me out."

• And only then... "What was that request again?" (And what is the charge code...?)

Whether politics translates into obstacle-making, backstabbing, or opportunism, it does get in the way. What might the reason be for politics, especially when it can be so hurtful and dysfunctional to the team?

It is a natural thing to not only do your job, but ensure that your manager knows that you did it. Unfortunately, some corporate cultures are so competitive that some employees believe that to get ahead requires winners (them) and losers (anyone else). At their worst, a Political Wolf's credo is "Take the credit and give the blame." Others play politics because they believe that stepping on others can only make them look better. Or they have such low self-esteem that only by being vicious to others can they feel satisfied themselves.

On the other hand, can politics be used productively? Political Wolves often have a heightened sense of awareness about how others think. Harnessing this capability to understand your manager's objectives is extremely useful. Harnessing this capability in a business development or networking context is equally important.

> Politics are a necessary part of any workplace. Whether they are good or bad, depends on how they are used.

Thankfully, a focused approach on delivering on your objectives – and developing strong relationships – can inoculate you against the negative effects of the Political Wolves. Recognize the behavior, and focus on delivering results – not spin.

IMAGE MANAGERS: Some people within the organization are more concerned about ego and personal positioning than the business. Perhaps they wear the flashiest clothes, or perhaps not. They are the ones who spend more time on how the PowerPoint presentation looks than on the content of the presentation itself. And they make sure to leave voicemails and emails for as many people as possible when they work on the weekend. While every organization needs its motivational speakers, and there is always a place for style, nobody should be left asking the question "Where's the beef?" Your clients are paying you for "beef," so make sure that you deliver!

ONE-DIMENSIONAL WONDERS: We sometimes find the One-Dimensional Wonder among the most driven "A-type" personalities. They are concerned only about work. They don't appear to have strong relationships beyond those at the office. They are so focused on the task that they forget the human element of their customers or their colleagues. When in a position of authority, they are often ruthless in their drive and alienate the very people they should be motivating. Their negative energy certainly gets things done, but it doesn't produce the "best" work environment.

THE STUPID ONES: Do you find yourself having to explain your requirements to your colleagues over and over to gain understanding? Does your patience wane when others don't "get it" as fast as you? While nobody is the perfect communicator, a tight labor market will mean that some of those who have been hired may not be as sharp (or as fluent) as you might like to see. If you are in a family business, nepotism doesn't help, either.

Learn from each of your colleagues, no matter their style.

Whatever the reason, you may be becoming frustrated by these people. They can be terribly efficient at developing roadblocks and preventing action.

Before jumping on the "Exactly!" bandwagon, here's a suggestion: consider that, just maybe, these people see you as patronizing and arrogant and are acting this way only to annoy you. Before accepting that your organization has the "Stupid Ones" problem, try to reason how you would both change others' perceptions of you and ultimately fix the problem. If you move to another group, a different firm, or a different industry altogether, the same issue may dodge you wherever you land; test-driving a solution immediately gives you invaluable experience.

THE HOARDERS: Several years ago, a salesperson in my organization told me, "Don't worry, Randall, the prospects will be calling in the next three weeks: my system works." Salespeople have used this line, or a version of it, forever. What is this much-vaunted system? It usually is a bunch of wheel-spinning, calls, faxes, and meetings, but unless there is transparency to the process, and until there are results, it is just smoke and mirrors. How can you deal with this obfuscation? Call them on it: tell them that the time of Secret Sauce is over, and they now have to open up and reveal their ingredients.

The salesperson in this example is a Hoarder. Hoarders seek to differentiate themselves with knowledge that no one else has. The disease strikes people throughout the organization, from people who hoard knowledge on a client to those who hoard knowledge about a product, a supplier relationship, a production machine, a piece of software, or even what's happening within the organization.

What if your boss is a Hoarder? Earlier in my career, I worked in a department run by one. The most senior executive had access to all information. In his schema, senior managers got less, and managers got even less. Analysts got pretty much nothing, and the support staff was pretty much invisible. All this information segregation, and there were only about 15 people in the group! Human nature being what it is, many people spent time guessing what was happening, filling in the blanks with worst-case scenarios, and making their decisions with incomplete data. A boss who is a Hoarder is particularly difficult – you're effectively being controlled by your lack of knowledge. A general rule: the more senior someone is, the more transparency is required. Unfortunately, the exact opposite is usually the case.

Hoarders value exclusive access to information.

Interestingly, Hoarders are the flip-side to one of the major advantages of a large organization: your unique knowledge adds value and makes you feel important. On the surface, it appears that when you hoard, it's good, but when others hoard, it's bad! If you think you may be a Hoarder yourself, remember too that being team-oriented is in, and Hoarders are not seen as team players.

SUMMARY: Are you a Hoarder, a One-Dimensional Wonder, a Political Wolf, or an Image Manager? Before you answer, consider that there are elements to each of these characters within each of us, and that's not a bad thing. And sometimes, it is important to put on one of these hats to achieve your objectives. A few examples: The fact that we're so concerned about image sets the bar higher for quality. Our political skills help us understand the dynamics with our clients. One-Dimensional Wonders push us to achieve more than we thought possible. Hoarders often become great repositories of corporate (and client) history. And so on.

FOCUS

- Process and people knowledge. Support systems. Multiple career paths. Security. Corporate name recognition. Are you prepared to make a change and possibly give them up? What would your days look like without IT support or without your assistant? How would you feel working for a company that didn't have a "name"? Or without the people that you've spent years working with? To a certain degree, each has contributed to your success. Before you decide that the grass is greener anywhere else, recognize what you currently have.

- Remember that career planning is not about change – it is about planning your career.

- Understanding your environment gives you the context to do this properly.

Chapter 4:
Today's Business Environment

CHAPTER IN A FLASH: *Your career doesn't happen in a vacuum: plan your career for today's (and tomorrow's) business environment. Learn from the past – don't repeat it.*

When layoffs, mergers and acquisitions, tighter financial scrutiny, and outsourcing all began to hit a number of years ago, many business magazines ran stories touting the end of employee loyalty. They were right, employee loyalty took a big hit – but it didn't end, it merely changed.

In the past, there was a quid pro quo: you looked out for the company, and in return the company looked out for you. My late grandfather's career was a perfect example of this. After high school he went to work in the back shop of a small manufacturing company. He worked hard and moved up the ranks quickly; when he retired forty-odd years later, he was a senior vice-president. He stayed at the company – Chrysler – his entire professional life.

Since this time, loyalty has become more complex. On one hand, you may feel an objective detachment about your employer; you've grown up, and you realize that there is no such thing as a job for life. You also recognize a new rule of corporate loyalty: the company can let you go, and you can choose when to move on yourself. While this sounds relatively uncomfortable, it speaks to the concept of employee empowerment and the critical importance of career planning.

On the other hand, most employees feel a great loyalty toward their colleagues. Think of your own situation: how you rely on your workmates and how they rely on you. The change from a hierarchical, authority-based management approach to a team-based one reinforces this new type of loyalty further.

As well, many take pride in being part of an organization that is professional, provides personal opportunity, and serves great clients. In many firms, there is a definite movement to foster stewardship well below senior ranks. All of these factors help the younger manager strive for achievement; loyalty is a by-product.

At the same time, there is less of a stigma to being laid off or deciding to switch careers. And if this happens, many organizations have well-developed alumni programs, designed to foster loyalty (and referral business) well after the departure.

Loyalty takes many forms: to your employer, to your manager, to your colleagues.

There are some people whose loyalty is driven exclusively by compensation. They typically will comment that everyone they know has moved at least once for more money. As we'll see later in the Job Quality Checklist, compensation is important, but it isn't the only reason people move – nor the most important. At this point, suffice it to say that if you fundamentally don't like your job, money won't change your mind.

Beyond loyalty, other changes in the business environment have occurred. Economic pressures have forced many organizations to become more effectively managed. This means that recruiting and retention, professional development programs, business accountability, and internal processes have matured considerably. From an individual's perspective, this is a double-edged sword: with greater conformity of processes, there is greater opportunity for development and personal growth. But with that conformity, unless you have gone through the career planning process yourself (and act on it), your career development will take you on the "default" path – which may not be as fulfilling as one you set yourself.

Changes in the business environment can have a profound impact on your career path. Consider the following observations on recent changes: how might each of these influence your development plans? And what other business issues and trends should you keep in mind?

- Speed to market matters, but there has to be a market that you're speeding to.
- Valuation should be done by the fundamentals – not by "eyeballs."
- A business plan has to be based on reality.
- The world is flat: ideas and work, not just capital, are borderless.
- Business ethics and personal credibility are the basis of the public trust: once they are lost, they cannot be regained.

What do these concepts have to do with career planning? Simple: as George Santayana, the notable philosopher, said, "Those who do not learn from history are doomed to repeat it." If you think the grass is greener on the other side, answer these questions: How does the organization define its market? How is the organization valued? What is the business planning process, and how often is it reviewed? What is the experience level of your future colleagues? And what is their track record and reputation in the marketplace?

Then answer these questions for your current employer. How do they stack up?

FOCUS

- The changes in the last several years have taught us many valuable lessons. Some relate to basic business fundamentals (rather than eyeballs), others relate to the importance of honesty and disclosure in financial statements.

- The challenge is to learn from our environment, not just observe it.

- The business environment is continuously changing – and your career plan should reflect and acknowledge these changes. Plan for the future, not the past.

- More money isn't necessarily the best measurement of success.

Chapter 5:
Assessment

CHAPTER IN A FLASH: *SkillChecks I and II help you identify your skills, your interests, and your gaps. Later in your career planning journey, you will use these results to identify activities to fill in any gaps. This chapter also introduces Reality Check Interviews – specific questions asked in special interviews that identify how others achieved success, and at what cost. During these interviews you will pick up a wider vocabulary to describe your personal strengths and capabilities.*

It may have been some time since you've considered where your strengths are. Yes, you started your career in one direction, but experience has broadened your exposure and you have grown considerably. An inventory of both your technical/analytical skills and your people/creative skills can help identify areas of weakness that require polishing and areas of strength that might be leveraged as you progress.

The reason for assessment is to help you identify the underlying skills (such as quantitative or analytical) that may be useful in a completely different venue. The analysis takes part in three sections.

SkillCheck I requires you to write answers to several questions, while SkillCheck II is a more traditional inventory. Try not to look at SkillCheck II until SkillCheck I is complete. The difference between this exercise and other market-based assessments is that these are not comparative: SkillChecks require a deeper personal introspection. The third section, Reality Check Interviews, does double duty: it provides an external perspective on ourselves, and it provides a window into the choices of (and results earned by) others.

SkillCheck I

Write three to five paragraphs for each of the following questions. If you would like a more challenging test, answer these questions longhand (or on the computer without using cut-copy-paste). This will force you to think through the answer in detail, before committing the proverbial pen-to-paper. You can type them into a computer for revisions and finesse later.

1. What is your educational and training background? (Include university, professional certifications, internal and external seminars)

2. Look back at your college or university transcripts. Was there a course that you found interesting, but you never did follow up or take more advanced training? Why was it interesting?

3. What specific skills did you hone to excellence in your previous three roles (or serving your last three clients)?

4. What aspects of your previous three roles provided the greatest satisfaction?

5. What areas of knowledge or skill do you see as your biggest weakness?

6. What non-work activities provide you the most satisfaction? What is it about these activities that interest you?

7. Which sections of the newspaper do you read first? Which magazines and online newsletters do you subscribe to?

Most organizations have their staff participate in an annual appraisal process. You set your objectives, review performance against the previous objectives, and find out how much you'll be paid the next year. Some firms will also spend some time with you on your career objectives. But the questions in SkillCheck I will rarely be asked, because the information they elicit tends to either be very far away (educational training) or transcends several jobs over time. The value of SkillCheck I is that it forces you to confront these questions directly. And in writing your answers, you have to spend time thinking.

SkillCheck II

SkillCheck II is a ranking of your knowledge and skills in a number of areas in business. Needless to say, it does not "dive deep" but is designed to enumerate skills across a broad spectrum of knowledge. For each skill type, rank yourself according to the following criteria:

BASIC: Some training or knowledge in the area, but requires updating (or mentoring) to work independently.

INTERMEDIATE: Knowledgeable, but may have difficulty taking a leadership role in the area, or Guru, but slightly out of date.

GURU: Expert and leader in the area, publicly recognized.

BLANK: If you have no training or knowledge in the area (yet), leave the Self-Assessment column blank.

Self Assessment: Basic/Intermediate/Guru	General Management and Miscellaneous
_____	Turnarounds and Restructuring
_____	Process Re-engineering
_____	Project Management
_____	Internal Consultant
_____	Business Unit Head
_____	Focus Group Facilitation
_____	Board-level Experience
_____	Corporate Secretary
_____	Legal Experience – Transactions
_____	Legal Experience – Advocacy
_____	Legal Experience – Policy
_____	Strategic Planning
_____	Sustainability
_____	Research and Development
_____	International Management _____
_____	Professional Certifications _____
_____	Other _____
	Sales
_____	Sales Management
_____	Sales Forecasting
_____	Sales (deals <100K)
_____	Sales (deals between 100K and 1M)
_____	Sales (deals >1M)
_____	Pre-sales Support
_____	Other _____

Finance and Accounting

_____ CFO
_____ Regulatory Compliance
_____ Corporate Finance – Banks and Other Lenders
_____ Corporate Finance – Public Markets/Regulatory Issues
_____ Investor Relations/Creditor Relations
_____ Audit – Public Companies
_____ Audit – Small and Medium-Sized Enterprises
_____ Internal Audit
_____ Treasury, Cash Management, Foreign Exchange
_____ Budgeting
_____ Performance measurement
_____ Controller, Accounting, Statement Preparation/Review
_____ Bookkeeping
_____ Management Accounting (including Activity-Based Costing)
_____ Valuations
_____ Financial Analysis
_____ Mergers, Acquisitions, and Divestitures
_____ Receivership and Insolvency
_____ Risk Management
_____ Forensic Accounting and Investigations
_____ Real Estate
_____ International Tax
_____ Corporate Tax
_____ Commodity Tax
_____ Personal Tax
_____ Financial Planning
_____ Financial Management Software (_____)
_____ Tax Software (_____)
_____ Other _____

MIS

_____ Senior IT Management (e.g., CIO or similar)
_____ Computer Audit
_____ IT Program Management
_____ Technical Architecture
_____ Programming, Network, and System-Related Functions
_____ Change Management
_____ Business Analyst
_____ Technical Writer
_____ Implementation of an ERP System
_____ Implementation of a CRM System
_____ Implementation of a Successful e-Commerce System
_____ Other _____

Marketing

_____	Advertising
_____	Market Research
_____	Product Development
_____	Brand Strategy
_____	Services Marketing
_____	Direct Marketing
_____	Internet Marketing
_____	Channel Management
_____	Corporate Identity
_____	CRM Software
_____	Media Relations/Public Relations
_____	Government Relations
_____	International Marketing
_____	Database Marketing
_____	Other _____

Manufacturing, Production, and Supply Chain

_____	Factory Management
_____	Quality Systems and Management
_____	ERP Software (_____)
_____	Logistics/Transportation
_____	Import/Export
_____	Purchasing
_____	Inventory Management
_____	Data Management
_____	Other _____

Human Resources

_____	Most Senior HR Manager
_____	HRIS Systems
_____	Payroll Systems
_____	Benefit and Pension Plans
_____	Compensation
_____	Recruitment
_____	HR Generalist
_____	Corporate Trainer
_____	Coaching/Mentoring
_____	Labor Negotiations
_____	Other _____

	Industry Vertical
_____	Retail
_____	Wholesale/Distributor
_____	Manufacturing
_____	Resource Sector
_____	Financial Services
_____	Professional Services
_____	Information Technology
_____	Telecom and Utilities
_____	Government/Public Services
_____	Non-Government/Non-profit Organizations
_____	Other _____

Okay, so you didn't actually do the two SkillChecks, did you? (Or maybe you just "scanned" them?) You want to get into the meat, and these exercises look like they would take a bit more time than you have right now? No problem. Just make sure that you actually do them, as the results will be used as a touchpoint several times throughout the career planning process. More reasons to do them now: SkillChecks help you better articulate your strengths to others and provide focus for how you spend your time. Remember you can't manage your career by passively reading a book – get yourself more fully engaged by actively going through these activities.

For those who completed the SkillChecks, the next task is analysis.

SkillCheck I is "you-centered": across your career, what you are good at, where you are weak, and what you enjoy doing. The value of SkillCheck I is in the thinking and doing. SkillCheck II, which is a bit more mechanical, puts your skills in context with others: how well do you know what you know.

ANALYZING SKILLCHECK I: Think through the areas that were easy to answer, and those that were more difficult. Spend a few moments considering why. Did some of your answers surprise you? You may find it useful to share your answers with your manager, a family member, or a close personal friend. Ask them if they see any surprises, or if they would have expected you to answer any of the questions differently.

> SkillChecks help you better articulate your strengths to others.

ANALYZING SKILLCHECK II: It is important to acknowledge your blind spots (or "gaps"), even though you may be uncertain of your future path. For example, you think you may be interested in biotech venture capital. A gap may exist if you have not yet developed skills in R&D, or if you do not understand the biotech industry. If you are a CFO looking at general management but haven't had experience in sales or marketing, there may be a gap here too.

Review the results of SkillCheck II. A gap exists wherever you have left your self-assessment blank or rated your level as basic. Ask yourself these questions about each gap:

- Are there gaps because you haven't ever been educated in the area before?

- Are there gaps because you have not yet had the opportunity to personally develop experience in the area? (Or because you've always shied away from trying?)

- Are there gaps because you really don't enjoy the area? (Or perhaps because you think that you wouldn't enjoy doing them?)

Gaps aren't "bad". No matter how clever you are, you can't know everything.

Gaps aren't "bad": no matter how clever you are, you can't know everything. Part of determining the nature of any future training or education is to look at your basics and blanks, determine what is required in your next role, and then develop a plan to fill in the gaps. The problem, of course, is that you may not know what is required in your next role. So how do you *develop the plan to fill in the gaps?*

The answer is simple: it doesn't matter if you don't know your exact future role; later in this book we'll return to this question. Use a proxy goal for now, and plan toward that proxy.[2] As you execute your plan and your thinking matures, you can always do a mid-course correction. When your goal is almost locked down, you can do yet another mid-course correction. And so on. The most important thing is not to do nothing: *do something that gets you moving approximately in the direction you want to go – and start doing it NOW!*

Of course, you will be successful in your career because of your strengths, not your gaps. Identifying your gaps merely helps you focus your time as you develop.

A real litmus test: ask your manager to rate you on each dimension of SkillCheck II, in order to compare their perception to yours.

---

2 A proxy is a placeholder. For example, assume you were interested in finance, but weren't sure whether you were interested in corporate finance, mergers and acquisitions, or commercial banking. Choosing a proxy goal of corporate finance will allow you to plan in the general direction of finance; as you learn more, your proxy can change to become more specific.

Reality Check Interviews

While the SkillChecks help us self-define our capabilities and interests, a lot can be gained by asking for an external perspective. There is also a lot to be learned by observing the impact of others' career choices.

Reality Check Interviews do this by looking at success from a different perspective: someone else's. What would the impact be of a different mix of priorities? We know about ourselves, because we live in our bodies and experience the impact of our decisions each and every day. But how have other people made similar decisions, as they chased their own success? And those decisions – have they paid off? What can you learn from them, and what advice might they give to you, if asked? Reality Check Interviews are called that because they are grounded in the real experiences of others.

The first step is to make a list of 30 people whom you see as being successful. These people, hopefully all with more years of experience than you, will have arrived at their current station in life through one path or another. They can be managers (current or former), entrepreneurs, corporate executives, politicians, clergy, publishers, or anyone whom you believe has a story to tell. Do not seek only those who know you well for this exercise. Those who know you only peripherally (or not at all) may **Most people** have had a unique career path, and their perspective could be **appreciate the** important to you as well. It may be tempting to interview only 10 to **opportunity to** 15 people, but push yourself for all 30. While finding 30 may be **share their** difficult, forcing this number ensures that the list goes beyond "the **experiences.** usual suspects," and that there is an appropriate (and wide enough) variety of experience to review.

The overall objective is to individually interview these people – for 30 minutes, 45 at the most – and ask them a series of questions that help you understand how they got to where they are now. A secondary objective is to ask them for feedback about you.

Process

- Explain the purpose of the meeting. You're approaching a turning point in your career, and you're meeting several senior people whom you see as successful; you'd like to understand how they got to where they did, and some of the reasons behind the choices they made. You wanted to take 30 minutes, 45 at the most, etc.

- I have found that interviewing the person for breakfast or lunch works better than meeting at their office, where distractions can cut the meeting short. (If you meet over a meal, don't be cheap – pick up the tab!)

- Don't ever tack this interview onto another reason for meeting. And don't bring anyone else to the meeting with you!

- When you meet with them, let them know that the conversation is private and confidential; ask if it is okay to take notes. It may help to imagine yourself as a newspaper reporter, dispassionately collecting facts for an article.

- After the interview, summarize your notes into a "meeting memo" for later reference.

- Send a thank you note.

Here is a list of questions to get you started. Note that they go from the general to the private. As people get more comfortable talking about themselves, they will reveal more sensitive (and therefore more valuable) information to you.

- Can you give me a rundown on your career?

- Did you get any "big breaks," or was there a specific turning point? Elaborate on the impact...

- Did you create any of these big breaks yourself? Elaborate on how...

- What was the best piece of advice your mentors gave you?

- If you could go back and re-do some of your decisions, what would they be?

- Were there any unexpected trade-offs that happened as a result of your success? (e.g., personal relationships, less community involvement)

- How active are you in your non-work activities – personal fitness, spirituality, education, etc.?

- How would you define *success*, generally? What grade (e.g., A-B-C-D-F) would you give yourself on the success scale?

- If you could rewind the clock, was there one thing you could have done that would have improved your grade?

Halfway through the meeting, change the focus from them to you. The questions you ask are determined by your relationship with them. For example, if someone knows you as a volunteer, their feedback will be through that lens. If they know you as a former workmate, their feedback will reflect their workplace experience with you. Of course, the better they know you, the more relevant their response. If they don't know you at all, modify the questions appropriately. Here are several of the *me* questions to get you started.

- You've known me in the capacity of _____; if you could put a label on my greatest strength, what would it be?
- What would you say my *blind side* was?
- Five years in the future, what type of role would you see me playing?
- What might you see as my first step in getting there?

These interviews are not designed to be "information interviews" of the sort used in job searches; they are to help you mature your own understanding of success.

Findings

While the results of each interview will be unique, there will be some common threads:

- You will begin to identify positively with some of the things that are said. You will also identify some of the problems you should avoid.

What is the most important lesson that each person "taught" you?

- People may lament that the cost of their success has been very high; often with spoiled personal relationships or poor personal health.

- After 20-odd interviews, many of the responses will start to sound familiar. As this starts to happen, you should begin feeling that your proxy goal is becoming more certain.

When you have completed all the Reality Check Interviews, spend time summarizing your meeting notes. What were the common attributes, positive and negative? What is the most important lesson that each person "taught" you during the interview?

FOCUS

Developing the discipline to go through these exercises provides two major benefits: (1) you learn more about yourself, and (2) you develop the discipline that will be critical as your career progresses.

ACTION CHECKLIST

❑ SkillCheck I
❑ SkillCheck II
❑ Reality Check Interview list
❑ Reality Check Interviews (and notes)

Work-Life Balance

Career Planning in Context: While having a great job is extremely important, most people work for a reason beyond the job itself: they work to live, not the other way around. When the balance gets upset, research shows that employee frustration increases, and employee retention worsens. Defining your balance isn't something that can be delegated to your manager, the HR department, or anyone else. Defining a unique personal "balance" is pivotal to the question of career planning itself.

Chapter 6:
The Personal Balance Sheet

CHAPTER IN A FLASH: *The term "work-life balance" is an inappropriate term of balance because of its binary nature. A more appropriate model is the Personal Balance Sheet; it uses the seven dimensions of Community, Family, Intellectual, Spiritual, Physical, Career, and Financial. Central to the theme of balance is that there is no such thing as a universal perfect balance – just a balance that each person can choose for him or herself.*

"Of course I'm successful – look at my car!" Not surprisingly, defining success generically is pretty much impossible, as each person has a uniquely personal view of the term itself. The Personal Balance Sheet is a productive model to use, as it defines the categories in which success may be found: Community, Family, Intellectual, Spiritual, Physical, Career, and Financial. Consider what each of these mean, and answer the following questions. Note the questions that resonate most with you, as these will provide clues later. Some of them may make you feel uncomfortable, while others are irrelevant to your world view. The idea is to help you define each dimension in your unique personal context.

COMMUNITY: What is your community profile? Do you know your neighbors? What have you contributed to the community you live in? Are you making an impact there? Do others recognize your contribution? Are you satisfied with the friendships you have outside the workplace? Do you care about the area where you live?

FAMILY: How good are your family relationships? Do you ever experience guilt over how much (or how little) time you spend with your family? How close is your extended family? Are you making a positive impact on the lives of your children, spouse, and parents? Do you have a spouse or life partner? Is your relationship growing closer, or is it languishing? Is family relevant to you at all?

INTELLECTUAL: Are you getting smarter, or are you feeling "dumber" each year? How many challenging non-fiction books do you read each year, outside of work-related titles? What non-work courses have you attended during the last year? Can you still do complex math in your head, or do you routinely look for a calculator or spreadsheet first?

SPIRITUAL: Do you regularly spend time contemplating spiritual ideas? Are you involved in any religious learning? Do you feel comfortable answering young children's questions about religion and spirituality? Do you feel guilty about not spending enough time in this area? Is spirituality relevant at all to you?

PHYSICAL: Do you feel unhealthy? Do you think you could be in better shape? Are you unhappy or embarrassed with the way your body looks? Does your doctor give you health advice (stop smoking, start jogging, lose weight, eat properly) that you don't follow to the letter? Is physical health relevant to you at all?

FINANCIAL: Do you think you are compensated appropriately, given your job and your efforts? Are you making as much money as you had expected to? Do you own your own house, car, boat, etc.? Do you worry about your level of debt? Are you saving enough for the future (e.g., house, children's education, retirement)?

CAREER: Has your career progressed to where you expected it to be by now? Do you have one or two close mentors? Do you feel you are in control of your career? If you had to do it all over again, would you have taken a different direction or done something else?

If asked publicly, most people would say that they are successful and might justify their success by pointing to their car, home, or job title. Privately though, I doubt many people are as happy as they want to be. Material possessions shouldn't define success, but for some people, they are a mistaken proxy for it. Remember: the point of career planning is to ensure that your *career* helps you achieve your *personal* goals, not the other way around. The following exercise helps make it happen for you.

Personal Balance Sheet

Before we even start, go through the questions above and write down your answers, even if it is in the margins of this book. (This exercise is more helpful if you are completely honest with yourself!)

Think back to the beginning of your career. What were your aspirations? Even if they were somewhat naive, those goals eventually led you to where you are today. Then think about the goals you had two years ago. Had your aspirations changed from when you started out? Likely they had, given the benefit of your experience.

Write these all down in the first two columns in the chart below.

Now, consider your "current status," and use the answers to the earlier questions to fill in the *current status* column. And finally, write down your next goal on the chart, before you move on. It is not critical to have your next goals locked down tight at this stage; you can always make changes later. Leave the last column (with the diamond) blank for now.

Personal Balance Sheet

Dimension of Success	Goal at start of career	Goal five years ago	Current status (answers to questions)	Your next "goal"	◆
Community					
Family					
Intellectual					
Spiritual					
Physical					
Financial					
Career					

Depending on your honesty, some of the Personal Balance Sheet may be very hard to fill out. If so, it is worthwhile asking yourself why. Had you not thought along these dimensions before? Or had your career planning and goal setting always been done in the context of your current employer, rather than in the context of "you"? Clarifying your next goal along these dimensions gives you a starting point for action.

If you have children, consider again your definition of balance. Since you are the closest example for your children to follow, it shouldn't surprise you when their balance choices begin to mirror your own. If you are physically fit, they probably will be too. If you missed their birthdays, don't be surprised if they miss yours. If they see you living an appropriately balanced life, not only do you benefit, they will too. The apple doesn't fall far from the tree.

DEFINING SUCCESS IS VERY PERSONAL. Some people may weight Career and Financial extremely high to the exclusion of all other attributes, while others may weight Family or Spiritual highest. There is no judgment on what is right or wrong: your priorities are purely a personal choice. And they will change with time, as we'll see in the next chapter.

FOCUS

- Career planning is an intensely personal activity. To achieve balance, your career should lead you toward your personal goals; your job shouldn't define who you are as a person.

- Work-life balance isn't a binary concept: The Personal Balance Sheet, like you, is multi-dimensional.

- Success is defined very personally along a number of dimensions: Community, Family, Intellectual, Spiritual, Physical, Financial, and Career. How do you stack up?

ACTION CHECKLIST

❑ Personal Balance Sheet

Chapter 7:
What Chapter Are You On?

CHAPTER IN A FLASH: *Each phase, or "chapter," of your life should have a different optimal balance. In fact, many balance problems are caused merely by living in one chapter, when you should really be in another. Balance is primarily your responsibility, but your friends, family, and employer aren't completely off the hook.*

While we've already defined balance in a more mature way using the Personal Balance Sheet, there is one dimension that we haven't discussed: time. Said another way, should the way you look at balance change as you change? (It should.)

A helpful way to look at balance is through the metaphor of chapters in a book. Each chapter has a different purpose and (usually) occurs at a different point in time. The early chapters introduce the main characters and set the scene. The middle chapters introduce some intrigue and develop relationships. And the end of the book reaches a climax as the mystery is solved.

If we consider how we live our lives, we also go through many phases, or chapters. A "traditional" book may look like this:

1. Parental dependence as a child

2. Discovery in college or university

3. Initial career

4. Commitment to a life partner ("Dual Income No Kids")

5. Mid-career and children

6. Empty-nesters

7. Retirement

Consider: What are the attributes typical of those in the initial career phases?

• Little or no family obligations

• Student loans outstanding

• Great desire to differentiate themselves from their peers and get promoted

During this phase (or "chapter") of life, an optimal Personal Balance Sheet may tilt fully toward Financial and Career, and perhaps very little to Community. Further along, if you have children, the Family dimension of the Personal Balance Sheet will increase in importance. Looking at a retiree, there may be no focus on Career and a huge focus on Family, Community, and perhaps Spiritual. As we move from one role to the next, we go through different "chapters" of our life, with different Personal Balance Sheet requirements.

Probably the most important Personal Balance Sheet insight is this: No one except you can properly define what the optimal balance is for you. Not your friends, not your mom, and certainly not your employer. The reason for this should be obvious: no one knows you better than you! Unfortunately, many individuals improperly expect their employer to provide balance – they can't, and if they tried, they'd likely guess wrong.

Those around you do, however, have an important role to play. Your family and friends must support you by understanding the balance choices that you have made (and, of course, the reverse is also true.) In fact, if you have a spouse or partner, the Personal Balance Sheet is a wonderful way to begin the discussion about priorities, and how to be supportive of the other's choices.

Your priorities will be different at different points in your life.

Your employer is not completely off the hook either: in their case, they should be providing an environment where balance can occur. The economic rationale for providing this, beyond employee satisfaction, is focused on two drivers: increased productivity and employee retention. Here are some typical initiatives that might exist at your workplace:

Common vocabulary: It certainly helps if everyone means the same thing when they use the same words. To most managers work-life balance is a binary concept: more of one means less of another. On the other hand, the Personal Balance Sheet vocabulary is multi-dimensional, and speaks to different personal and organizational responsibilities.

Great management: This is developed through mentoring, formal training programs, and by example on-the-job. A great manager can properly balance the needs of the business with the needs of the individual. (Of course, poor management has implications well beyond work-life balance; in fact, research suggests that people don't quit their company, they quit their boss.)

Formalized "balance" programs: Best-of-class balance programs are designed to develop common vocabulary within an organization, help individuals design a balance that is best for them, and help individuals translate their plan into action. Unfortunately, many seminars on work-life balance are really no more than training on time management and stress management. (These are important skills to develop, but they deal more with the symptoms of poor balance, than solving the problems at the root.)

Alternative work arrangements: Sometimes these are institutionalized as "programs," and sometimes they are negotiated on an individual basis: job-sharing, flex-time, reduced work schedules, and seasonal schedules.

Family-friendly work arrangements: This might include work-from-home policies, on-site daycare, emergency daycare, and paid extended maternity/paternity/adoption leaves.

Employee assistance programs: In a time of change, professional counsellors provide perspective or connections to resources (such as lists of daycare alternatives, bereavement counselling, etc.).

Wellness programs: A host of initiatives are clustered under this umbrella, including alternative medical benefits, subsidized fitness memberships, nutritional counselling, and more flexible disability policies. There is a recognition that a healthy employee is a productive employee – and that when there isn't wellness, there is distraction.

Concierge and personal assistant services: Some organizations will arrange for personal errands to be done in order to provide greater focus on the job. These might be tasks as diverse as delivering dry cleaning, house cleaning, picking up children, or reserving sports tickets.

Other initiatives and benefits: These might include support for community involvement, meal plans, financial planning seminars, time off for religious observance, sabbaticals, and educational subsidies.

Often, there is a balance problem when we are still living in Chapter One, but should be in Chapter Three or Four. The solution is to complete the Personal Balance Sheet for the "right" chapter: the one we are currently on.

But still, why were we on that earlier chapter? Why didn't we dynamically "change" the chapter (and therefore our balance) over time?

People are creatures of habit, and we feel comfortable with... the routines we feel comfortable with: in this case, with Chapter One. And when we did think about changing balance, we have (until now) only thought about it in terms of the binary *work* or *life*. Might this be the case with you? If so, you're not alone.

This same concept – chapters – can apply within the year as well. Are certain months (busy season, quarter-ends, etc.) crazy-busy, while other times are lighter? There is no reason you cannot define your optimal Personal Balance Sheet to be different, depending on the season.

Earlier in this book, you completed the Reality Check Interviews to gain an external perspective on your skills. And in the previous chapter, you completed the first part of the Personal Balance Sheet. As should be clearly obvious by now, the Personal Balance Sheet choices made by your interviewees had a great impact on their success and on their happiness. What can you learn from their experience? Close the loop by going back to your Personal Balance Sheet. Make three additions:

1. **REVIEW THE REALITY CHECK INTERVIEW NOTES.** If you could summarize the top five "Balance Rules to Live By," what would they be?

2. **REVIEW YOUR PERSONAL BALANCE SHEET CURRENT GOALS.** Do they still make sense to you, given what you've learned in the Reality Check Interviews? You may want to refine and possibly modify them as a result. Make sure your goals are both practical and attainable within the next 12 to 18 months.

3. **ADD ANOTHER COLUMN ENTITLED CRITERIA FOR SUCCESS.** (In the Personal Balance Sheet, use the blank column headed by a diamond for this.) Based on what you've learned, how do you now define success for each dimension? These should be longer-term criteria. Answer the question: "I'll know I am successful in my [family, financial, etc.] life when _____".

FOCUS

There is a time dimension to balance; every time your life goes into a new "chapter," your Personal Balance Sheet will likely change.

ACTION CHECKLIST

❑ What chapter are you currently on? When might it change?

❑ Reality Check Interview Notes: *Top 5 Balance Rules to Live By*.

❑ Personal Balance Sheet: Add a column entitled Criteria for Success.

Chapter 8:
Don't Be Your Day Job!

CHAPTER IN A FLASH: *Learn how to compartmentalize your day by not "being" your job after hours. One technique is to introduce yourself using Personal Balance Sheet concepts.*

Now that you have completed your Personal Balance Sheet and have better clarity on *your* definition of balance, it is time to revisit one of the characters we described earlier in this book: the *One-Dimensional Wonder*. This is the worker who is solely focused on work, to the exclusion of everything else. Even though the Reality Check Interviews and the Personal Balance Sheet may have softened you a bit, how can you tell whether you are (or are becoming) a One-Dimensional Wonder?

As an experiment, when you next go out with non-work friends, count how many times you bring up a work-related topic. And how many times your friends do so. A tougher test: how many times during a social occasion do you have work-related issues on your mind? And when you meet someone in a social setting for the first time, how do you introduce yourself: as "a banker with XYZ"… or by a non-work trait?

When you define yourself solely on the basis of your job, and your job disappears, there is a problem: your self-image often disappears too. This predicament, usually felt by people who are fired, is really a symptom of a poor work-life balance. Once you are comfortable defining yourself beyond your job, even if nothing else changes, your balance attitude will begin to shift. Get into the habit *now* of introducing yourself socially without mentioning your work. How? Here's a hint: describe yourself using the other Personal Balance Sheet dimensions. At the start, try to memorize your introduction.

Certainly in North America, the introductory conversation is both formulaic and predictable. I say, "Hello, my name is Randall Craig. What is your name?" After you answer, I ask, "And what do you do?" In a pure business environment, the answer is standard: "I am a consultant at Pinetree Advisors …" We're asked what our day job is, and we answer. The problem occurs when we are in a purely social or semi-social networking environment. We don't want to answer "I'm my day job," but that is typically what happens. What are the alternatives?

As I was doing my MBA 15 or so years ago, I became quite friendly with one of my groupmates. Eventually, I invited her and her husband to dinner. After asking her husband his name (Mikey), I asked him what he did. His answer was brilliant: "I'm in manufacturing, but I spend a lot of my time long-distance cycling."

What is your answer to the question?

- "I'm in accounting, but I spent last year training for a marathon."
- "I'm in law, but I run a band on the weekends."
- "I'm in consulting, but my real passion is Japanese culture."

When someone asks the question, they usually aren't interested in finding out your exact title, client responsibilities, or year of graduation. They are merely looking to establish relationship and commonality. The technique of generalizing away from the specific ("I'm in accounting") and then redirecting toward a personal topic of interest (marathon training), sets the start of the relationship on a very different footing. And not automatically about your job.

If you aren't your day job, don't introduce yourself to others that way.

How do you know what topic of interest to choose? Start from your Personal Balance Sheet, and then choose a topic that you think might be of interest to the other person. This is a valuable insight as you begin to network with others. Over time, it will be these strong personal relationships that will turn into new opportunities.

I tell the story about Mikey whenever I speak to groups about work-life balance. A few years ago I was speaking with him (we're still good friends) and shared with him his claim to fame. I also told him that over a decade later, I *still* didn't know what he did for a living. He asked me why I didn't just ask. I told him I did ask on many occasions, but his answer was always a variation on a theme: "I'm in the furniture business, but I spend my real time as a community leader." "I'm in operations, but my real passion is…" I told him I didn't want to know his exact job, otherwise I couldn't honestly keep telling the story! And by this time in our relationship, it didn't really matter.

FOCUS

As you interact with people in your day-to-day life, avoid defining yourself in terms of your day job.

ACTION CHECKLIST

❏ Write down and practice your answer to the question "What do you do…", just like Mikey.

Developing Your Career

You may have thought to yourself once that if "it" happens one more time, you are going to quit. Or maybe a recruiter gets your name, dangles a great job plum in front of your nose, and begins to convince you that this is an opportunity of a lifetime.

In the first case you are running from a job, with no consideration of what you are running to. In the second case, you are running to a job, with no consideration of what you are leaving, and no consideration for any other alternatives within your present workplace. In either case, there is no benchmark for comparison.

How do you react when you see those appointment notices in the business paper? Is it envy, or do you convince yourself that the person is "lucky"? The reality is that luck has very little to do with it. Successful people create their own opportunities by being aware of their goals, continuously developing their skills and networks, and logically building their careers.

You may have noticed that the Personal Balance Sheet was the first major concept introduced in this book. The reason is simple: for the vast majority of people, the career tail should not be wagging the balance dog. Only once you've defined your Personal Balance Sheet goals can you evaluate whether a particular job is helping you achieve them.

Chapter 9:
Job Quality Checklist

CHAPTER IN A FLASH: *The Job Quality Checklist is a thought-starter for the specific activities that you will later do when executing your career plan.*

The Job Quality Checklist is an easy diagnostic tool that helps you take stock of your current role. Answering yes or no to six easy questions gives you a barometer on your current position – and easy criteria for your next.

1. Are you still having fun?
2. Are you being challenged intellectually?
3. Do you like your colleagues?
4. Are you reaching your career goals?
5. Are you achieving life balance?
6. Is your compensation somewhat close to your worth?

While you might be able to think of several other important questions, answering these ones first will provide perspective – and objective data points for your career development plans.

1. Still Having Fun?

When you wake up in the morning, are you actually excited about going into work and looking forward to getting there? Or has work slowly become less and less fun? Do you still get an intrinsic satisfaction going through "the process"?

You spend more time at your day job than anywhere else in life. You may as well enjoy yourself.

If your attitude toward your job has changed, what was it that caused the change? Perhaps the chase was exciting, but now that you've arrived, you're not exactly thrilled with the destination. Or maybe a particular event has changed your attitude.

I must admit that lying in the dentist's chair is not at all my idea of having fun. In fact, it is pretty much my least desired activity of all. Yet why do I go back, over and over through the years? Because my teeth are important, and it's worth the discomfort. If your job brings you no joy, better make sure the money is worth it.

As easy as "Still having fun?" sounds, it is tough to answer honestly, as we often justify our answers after the fact. To start your thinking process, try answering the following six questions:

- If you could choose any job in the world, would it be the one that you're in right now?
- Do you get out of bed each morning, excited about going to the office?
- Do you find yourself arriving later than you did years before and leaving earlier?
- Is the working atmosphere positive and exciting or negative and gloomy?
- Do you worry about work issues beyond the working day, and find that you cannot detach yourself from them?
- Ask the people closest to you: "Do you think that I am having fun at work? Am I excited about it? Do you think I would be happier elsewhere?"

Most people don't go to their jobs to have fun; some even rationalize this by saying that work and play are mutually exclusive activities. But unless you enjoy each day, you are missing a significant part of life.

2. Are You Being Challenged Intellectually?

We spend the first 18 years of our life sitting in school classrooms. We then spend a number of years in college or university; many of us pursue graduate degrees and professional certifications on top of that. Then we enter the workforce and exchange our *learning* hat for an *earning* one. Why should the learning stop after school? Enlightened organizations require all staff to participate in some sort of training each year, regardless of professional certification requirements.

But even if you attend training and professional development courses, it doesn't mean that your job itself provides intellectual challenge. In other words, do you have to use your head to do your job? For me, intellectual challenge means that I must always be learning. Others find intellectual challenge by being exposed to constantly changing technology or constantly changing professional standards. For you, the intellectual challenge must be… appropriate for you.

Intellectual strength becomes important if you are thinking of a promotion or other job change.

While intellectual challenge may not be such a high priority for everyone, a job that provides continuous intellectual challenge keeps you interested in the day-to-day. It also prevents you from "feeling dumb" over the years.

More importantly, though, is that intellectual challenge gives you the flexibility to deal with change. And if you are thinking of successfully moving up in your career, you *will need* that flexibility.

3. Do You Like Your Colleagues?

When you pick your friends, you pretty much have complete latitude. If you don't like someone (or they don't like you), you just don't spend time together. In the workplace, it's not so simple: you're thrown together and must work to meet common objectives.

Your job is a lot more pleasant when you enjoy working with your colleagues. It is far easier to get things done when you have a positive relationship with your manager, co-workers, and staff. It reduces the negative politics considerably and, when you're in a bind, gives you people to call upon.

Are your colleagues great role models, or poor ones?

"Do you like your colleagues?" doesn't mean that you have to be close personal friends. Nor does it mean that you have to be strong political allies. And it certainly doesn't mean currying favor with others so *they* like *you*.

It speaks to your colleagues as models. As you spend more time together, you will start taking on some of your colleagues' attributes, and they yours. Didn't like how rude everyone was when you started your job? Look in the mirror several years later: you have probably become ruder too! On the other hand, if your colleagues are excellent analysts, or great with relationships, you will pick up these skills too.

One way to assess the value of your colleagues as models is to answer this question: What is the most important positive and the most negative thing that I have learned from each of them?

Now, try substituting the word "boss" for colleague. Your boss can clear the way for you politically and improve your standing in the organization; a boss's word can result in promotion and better compensation. A good boss can act as a mentor or coach.

What happens if you have a bad boss? Should you leave or should you stay? Surely if you are beginning to despise your time at work, you might consider a change. But does the change mean leaving altogether, or merely moving to another position within the organization?

4. Are You Reaching Your Career Goals?

Your company has many stakeholders, including shareholders, customers, suppliers, employees, and perhaps also the general public. As it tries to satisfy all these groups, it is pretty much impossible to hit a "bull's eye" each time and for each group. For employees, bonus plans, objective-setting, and profit-sharing can generate some degree of alignment and stewardship. But with the exception of sole proprietorships and closely held partnerships, an organization's goals are rarely 100% aligned with those of any one particular individual.

Given this reality, how do you assess whether your current job is heading *you* toward *your* goals?

Think of your career plan as a broad path, going in a particular direction. Then think of a particular trajectory within that broad path: that is the direction your current job is taking you.

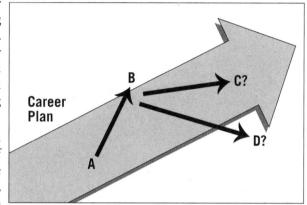

The diagram shows you at point A – the start of your last "job" within the organization. At point B, your current job is about to take you off your desired career path. Perhaps you are in a staff position but feel that you should be in a line position. In any case, if you keep on the same trajectory, you would not be in alignment and would eventually become frustrated. If you were to switch jobs at point B, one of your considerations should be whether your new job takes you to point C or D. The greater the alignment, the faster you achieve your goals, and more likely, the greater your satisfaction.

At point B, however, you can make another decision. You may wish to re-evaluate your career plan altogether and re-orient it to be in the direction of your current job. In this case, neither C nor D would make any sense, and you should look around for a position like one at point E. I should point out that job E might be the same as your current one, but with additional responsibilities. Or it might be the same job, but serving a different type of client. Or it might be outside of the organization completely.

Here's an example. Suppose you joined the company two years ago as an internal auditor, with the goal of eventually becoming the treasurer. You have recently been appointed as the manager in charge of receivables in their finance department; a job in treasury would be the next step for you. Meanwhile, another job opportunity comes up, running the finance department for a small subsidiary. Should you take it? If you do, you won't get the experience necessary for the treasury job. But on the other hand, running an entire department sounds fascinating and might mean even greater opportunity in the future. The decision is about a job – but also about your direction.

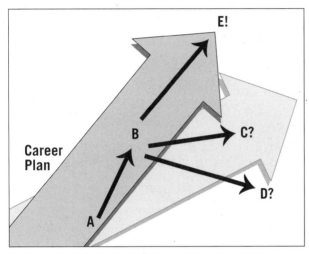

Remember that your career, and the jobs you take within it, is based on decisions that are yours to make. It doesn't matter whether you keep your career direction the same (e.g., job C or D), or choose to re-orient your career direction (and therefore take job E), so long as the choice you make is one that is made deliberately.

What should you do if you don't even have a career direction? Or if you feel you have been going in circles? Once again, consider the idea of a proxy goal, in approximately the direction you are interested in. If nothing else, this will give you a benchmark for comparison with your current job.

5. Are You Achieving Life Balance?

Reflecting on our accomplishments and successes, we can often attribute them to our strong work ethic: never saying no to new responsibility; going the extra mile for that important client; working through the night to get the proposal just right. However, success sometimes means making compromises along the way. Excessive travel. Neglecting fitness and health. Having little or no time for hobbies and volunteer activities. And spending less time with your family.

At different times in your life, there may be different priorities, and near the beginning of your career, your first priority is likely to be... your career. However, after this initial push to establish yourself, there should be a movement toward a different balance; without it, you will pay a steep price, often in ways that are hard to foresee.

A former colleague of mine was known to be able to "fix" just about any project that had gone off the rails. He had fun on each of his assignments, and he did find them challenging. He was working with people he liked, and each assignment raised his profile in the company. He certainly was paid well enough. Unfortunately, each assignment also had one other thing in common: it took about 18 hours each day, six days a week, for about three months. As one can expect, this schedule didn't leave time for much else. After many years of working like this, he realized he had missed much of his children's formative years – a steep price indeed, paid by him and his children. He also paid the price with his health, taking stress leave several times over the years.

As you went through the Reality Check Interviews, you may have run across similar stories. My former colleague's problem was that he hadn't considered the chapter he should be on; he forgot to change the chapter. He should have realized that when his children were of a certain age, his optimal balance should have changed: he could have changed the mix of the assignments he accepted.

Does your current job allow you to have the balance you desire?

Here's another reason for completing the Personal Balance Sheet exercise before looking at the Job Quality Checklist: once you've determined your desired balance, you can then more objectively look at how to achieve that balance within the context of your job and your career.

The question "Are you achieving life balance?" asks whether your current job provides you the opportunity to have your desired balance within the current chapter of your life.

Before you quickly answer "yes" or "no" about balance (or lack of it) in your current position, consider the word *opportunity*. You may find that your job provides the opportunity, but you have not yet figured out how to hook into it. Quick check: look at your peers and those slightly more senior than you are. Which of them have engaged the balance opportunity? Spend some time with them – they have something very important to teach you.

6. Is Your Compensation Somewhat Close to Your Worth?

Thankfully, the sophistication of compensation plans has improved dramatically over the last number of years. We're rewarded for individual performance. We're rewarded for team performance. We're rewarded for corporate performance. And less so (thankfully), we're no longer rewarded for merely having a pulse. Of course, many organizations still have a way to go, but most progressive organizations recognize that to retain their best, they must take the compensation issue off the table.

Even so, many of us aren't exactly certain we're paid enough, given our efforts. So how do we pin down exactly what we're worth? The answer is that we can't. The correct question is simply "Are we paid somewhat close to our 'worth'?"

To answer that question, answer these:

- Do you have enough income to provide for life's necessities?
- Is your compensation plan plus or minus 15% of others doing comparable jobs within the organization?
- Have you been approached *for the same job at a comparable employer*, with a compensation plan within 15% of your current plan?
- If the organization replaced you, how much would they have to pay?
- Based on available salary surveys, are you in the bottom quartile of pay, yet are a recognized star performer within your organization?

This "compensation" attribute should be in the Job Quality Checklist, but should only be looked at last. If you're paid a bit too little, think of it as an investment in your managerial training. If you're paid too much, perhaps it is to make up for a deficiency in the other attributes. In any case, the compensation plan shouldn't be your primary career planning driver – the other attributes are.

Sometimes it is worth taking a great opportunity, and letting the compensation catch up later.

While travelling on a long flight, I started a conversation with my neighbor on this very topic. Or rather, he started a conversation with me. He was an engineer who had left his job in an engineering firm to start a diagnostic device company. After five years of hard work, his decision is now just starting to pay off. His perspective on job change? Your new compensation must be high enough to account for the new risks in the other dimensions. How high? His number was 50%.

———⟫◆⟪———

How did you do on the Job Quality Checklist? If you didn't do well, don't feel too bad – and don't quit your job. The Job Quality Checklist is designed to identify red flags more than anything else. Once you know where there is a deficiency, you can take steps to fill in the gaps. You'll learn how in Chapter 14.

FOCUS

Is it the right time to consider change or not? If you were unhappy with your Job Quality Checklist answers, this should motivate you to do something about it: fill in the gaps.

ACTION CHECKLIST

❏ Job Quality Checklist

Chapter 10:
Collect Experience

CHAPTER IN A FLASH: *Learn about how to develop the critical experiences you will need in order to earn your next assignment.*

When I was first promoted to the rank of manager, I was proud of my accomplishment. Finally, a great title, a raise, and my golf club fees were being paid (they did that back then). I asked my boss how he had decided to promote me. His answer was excellent and reflected a truth that was clearly common sense. "Randall, I could promote you to a manager because you already were a manager."

When I looked at the work that other managers were doing, I saw that their responsibilities weren't all too different from mine. When you apply for a job, either internally or externally, the number one question on the mind of the hiring manager (or recruiter) is this: Has this person done this before?

Experiences are earned on and off the job.

The implication of this is profound. If you are to be considered for more senior roles anywhere, your job, right now, is to collect experiences that provide evidence of your capability. Getting promoted (or hired) isn't a *goal* of career development – it's the other way around. As career development happens, promotions are merely milestones along the way.

Note that the concept of collecting experiences is different than getting "experience." Experiences happen through a number of activities, on and off the job. At the end of the chapter is a partial list.

Within many Human Resources departments, this type of list is sometimes characterized as *Job Enrichment* opportunities. It is absolutely true that doing these activities will enrich the job that you are doing, develop broader perspective, and increase your value to the organization. We refer to them as career development activities only because collecting these experiences can also help you achieve your career development goals beyond your current role.

Another way to look at this list is from the perspective of the Personal Balance Sheet. Fully half of the list can be obtained through activities rightfully characterized as *Community, Family, Intellectual, Physical,* or *Spiritual*. Again, work-life balance is *not* binary: activities that you do outside of your work can have a dramatic – and specific – benefit to your progression on the job. We'll develop this theme further on in the book in the context of networking and business development skills.

At this time, you have hopefully completed the frameworks (Personal Balance Sheet, Reality Check Interviews, and Job Quality Checklist). **Before you go further,** choose one Internal activity, and one External activity from the list below, and add them to your calendar. Even if you are just skimming this book on a first go-round, remember that the goal of career planning is not to produce *thoughts*, but action.

Internal experience ideas	External experience ideas
• Actively participate in meetings	• Association membership
• Attend or deliver lunch and learn sessions	• Attend industry or trade conferences
• Beyond-the-job extra duties	• Attend part-time university (MBA?)
• Client and internal presentations	• Director on condo board
• Cross-training for different roles	• Earn an additional professional designation
• Discussions with your manager re goals/new projects	• Join Toastmasters
• Document business processes	• Membership on regulatory bodies
• Feedback from peers	• Mentor: find an external one for yourself
• Find efficiencies in assigned tasks	• Networking
• Job rotation	• Online newsgroups/forums
• Job shadowing	• Online professional development
• Look for models among your colleagues	• Organize activities for your school alumni
• Mentor: be one!	• Presentations to regulators or government
• Mentor: find one for yourself	• Read current business books
• Serve clients in different industries	• Read international publications
• Special projects, secondments, or seasonal transfers	• Read the newspaper each day
• Test new technology prior to roll-out	• Research a topic of interest
• Training courses	• Seminars: attend or deliver
• Update yourself on procedures, regulations, etc.	• Sports teams: participate or coach
• Webmaster for your group	• Trade journals: read, or contribute
• Work events and receptions	• Vacation in different countries
• Write status reports for managers	• Volunteer in a leadership capacity with a non-profit
• Write white papers	

FOCUS

- There are many ways to collect experience – and the majority are under your control.

- You can develop yourself and achieve something for your organization at the same time.

ACTION CHECKLIST

❏ What other activities might you put on the list from this chapter?

❏ Choose at least one activity from each column, and add them to your calendar for action.

Chapter 11:
Career Possibilities

CHAPTER IN A FLASH: *Learn about 17 different career possibilities. While many might not hold personal interest at the present time, it could be that they will several years from now. The chapter discusses how to use triggering events as a way to spur action on your part.*

At some point in your career, you will ask yourself whether the path you have chosen is the right one for you. Truthfully, the earlier you ask this question, the healthier your career will be. This is so because mid-course corrections are far easier in the first third of your career than the last. As career planning becomes a comfortable skill, mid-course corrections will become far easier to make, less traumatic, and less dramatic. Career revolution will give way to career evolution.

With the question of path comes the question of alternatives. In this chapter, you will be introduced to many different types of jobs. Some will hold appeal, and some will be irrelevant. Particularly if you are having challenges in your current role, try not to romanticize the more appealing alternatives. Developing a minimum level of success (and a modicum of excellence) demands tough work, sometimes endless tedium, and sometimes huge risk.

Recall this book's introduction: career *planning* is not synonymous with career *change*. While people do make changes throughout their career, many are already on the right path. For this large group, career planning means developing a deeper, broader, stronger understanding in their area of personal expertise. Don't let the wide variety of alternatives persuade you that somehow career planning requires career change: it doesn't.

Seventeen Career Possibilities
• Maintain the course
• New field/practice, industry, or function
• Staff rotations
• Non-traditional work arrangements
• Sabbaticals
• Join a client
• Move to Government, Regulator, Institute, Association, etc.
• Boomerang/Returnee
• Start-up/Entrepreneur
• Consultancy/Free Agent
• Purchase an Existing Business
• Trading Up: Working at another large organization
• Trading Down: Working at a smaller organization
• Earn a grad degree or professional certification (full or part-time)
• Volunteer/Community service work
• Stay at home with kids or parents
• Do something non-traditional

Maintain the Course

If you have done well in the Job Quality Checklist, maintaining the Status Quo isn't a bad choice. Continue doing what you're doing, and eventually you will end up at the correct level within your organization. That doesn't mean you shouldn't engage in career planning. And it doesn't mean that you can't do better with your Personal Balance Sheet.

Interestingly, all of the career development activities that you do to maintain your success within the organization, including professional development, networking/business development, service excellence, etc., are precisely the activities that will help you be successful outside – there is no downside in investing in yourself.

For many people, however, maintaining the course is the default option, merely because career planning is an unfamiliar activity: they go through their careers sleeping, allowing the prevailing wind to move them along.

Because of the hierarchical structure of many organizations, at some point the majority of those entering will leave – most voluntarily, some not so. These "sleepers," however, are rudely awoken when they realize that the next step for them may be *out*, instead of *up*. **Career insight**: When you *choose* to stay, you will be far more successful than those who stay by default.

Maintaining the course, however, doesn't mean doing nothing. It may mean developing your expertise to a deeper level. Or it may mean preparing yourself to merit a promotion.

I have spoken to many individuals over the years who have been upset about not getting a promotion. Usually when this happens, it shouldn't come as a surprise at all. Recall my manager's words? "I promoted you to manager because you already were a manager." If you quack like a duck, and they are looking for a duck, then you're in luck.

No one will give you a promotion: it must be earned. Once you are at that new level – whatever your title – it will be apparent to everyone: your manager with regard to promotion eligibility, and to recruiters in the case of external opportunities. Here are some ideas to help with getting promoted. None of these are rocket science, but they are too easily forgotten:

1. **ATTITUDE:** More than anything else, having a positive attitude can make a difference. As a simple example, think about your workmates you most enjoy being around, and those you don't. Negative attitudes

are demotivating and are not likely to win you any friends. A positive attitude will help "attract" the special projects – and recognition.

2. **DELIVER:** It is no longer about meeting your commitments, but exceeding them. When you make a promise, over-deliver on it. When you are given job objectives, over-deliver on them. Always exceeding your manager's expectations is a great way to demonstrate that you are able to handle more and that you always keep your word. Of course, managing your manager's expectations is a critical prerequisite.

Maintaining the Course shouldn't be the default; it needs to be a positive choice.

3. **CRITERIA:** Many organizations have specific requirements for promotion: a number of years at a previous level, annual goals being met, etc. These criteria are often *entrance criteria* for the next job: if you achieve them, you are eligible for consideration. If you haven't yet achieved the goals, you might be precluded from even applying. Once you know the criteria, you can fill in the gaps with education, special projects, or whatever is required. Asking also sets an expectation: it indicates you are interested in being promoted, and you will do whatever it takes to earn it.

4. **EDUCATION:** Are you currently enrolled in a program for an additional certification? When was the last time that you took a course, seminar, or workshop? Are you officially "qualified" to do that new job? And from a competitive perspective, do all of the new hires at your workplace have more recent knowledge than you? Continuous education is a key way to remain current – and remain competitive.

5. **CREDIT-SHARING:** If you don't share your successes on the way up, you won't have any support when you get there. And with today's mantra of "Team team team," those who don't share credit can easily disqualify themselves from promotion.

6. **NETWORK:** Your network is invaluable, as it can identify opportunities – and provide key support. Networking isn't about increasing your collection of business cards. It means getting to know the people who gave them to you, then actively doing things to help them. Think of your network like a bank account: you can't make a withdrawal from it without first making a number of deposits. And you can't expect others to help you unless you first help them. Later, in Chapter 17, we will develop this concept, Give to Get, much further.

7. **MENTOR:** Is there anyone in your workplace that you can help? Teachers often say that they learn more by being the teacher than the

student. Put this to the test – and simultaneously develop an internal group of supporters. Then develop your "mentee" relationships with those more senior than you. The feedback and guidance that you receive will smooth your way to the top.

8. **DRESS:** Consider the image you are portraying to those around you: are you dressing for the role that you're currently in, or the one you aspire to? While this may seem to be such a minor thing, your staff, peers, and managers make quick judgments about your capabilities based on your image – and clothing forms an important part of this. This concept, Personal Branding, is explored further in Chapter 20: Dress for Success!

9. **DE-STRESS:** Don't be so single-minded about the short-term promotion: relax, do your current job well, focus on continuous improvement, and enjoy your life. In a career that spans 30 to 40 years, if you are promoted one year later, will it really make such a huge difference? Review your Personal Balance Sheet commitments. You spend more time at your day job than doing anything else – you should enjoy yourself along the way.

10. **QUACK LIKE A DUCK:** Look at the successful people in your organization, and learn how they "quack." If you are able to model their successful attributes, you'll be one step closer to moving up to the next level.

Finally, if a position you're interested in is posted, apply for the role, with your manager's support.

What if you were hoping for a promotion and you were passed over? It is human nature to feel disappointment, and then want to put the whole event completely behind you. Unfortunately, when this is done, it also precludes the very healthy process of introspection.

If you do get turned down, use this same list, and ask yourself honestly whether you were firing on all ten cylinders. Were there things that you could have (or should have) been doing that you weren't? If so, make sure you start doing them now.

New Field/Practice, New Industry, New Function

Considering the huge investment that the firm has made in you, and the credibility that you have earned there, why quit if all you really want to do is change roles? By staying within the same organization, you don't give up seniority, you maintain your internal networks, and you avoid the wasteful "start-up" learning costs of a new organization. You can avoid taking one step back before taking one step forward.

If you consider your current role to be at an intersection of a number of different roads, changing just one (or two) roads is definitely easier than changing many. For example, you may be described along the following roads:

- Accountant with…
- Six years experience doing…
- Audits serving…
- Public companies in the…
- Food…
- Manufacturing business in…
- Canada, with…
- Multinational suppliers.

At the same time, you may also travel on a number of personal roads…

- Board member and marketing chair of the ABC Cancer Foundation
- Partially completed MBA
- Marathon runner
- Concert pianist

Changing only one or two of these attributes will yield different opportunities – all within the same organization. For example:

- Instead of Audit, consider opportunities in Tax, Forensics, Receivership & Insolvency, Mergers and Acquisitions, Valuations, etc.
- Instead of public companies, why not serve a different type of clientele: governments, regulatory agencies, not-for-profits, or independent businesses.
- Instead of the Food industry, why not serve clients in other industries?
- Instead of the Manufacturing business, why not serve clients either upstream or downstream: importers, distributors, retailers, etc.?
- Instead of working in this country, why not arrange for a year somewhere else, doing the same thing in a different jurisdiction?
- And finally, if you are going to change any of the above, why not marry it with some of your personal interests: music, health care, or the world of fitness?

Each of your strengths represents a unique career opportunity.

These changes are much more likely within the scope of your current organization, because of the credibility and reputation that you have built. And also because your employer wants to see a return on the investment they have made in you.

A short delay allows you to prepare for your new role.

That being said, instant transfers cannot always happen. The firm may have made a commitment to a client, and the timing might not be right. There may not be an opening in the area that you are interested in. There may be an issue with budget timing. Or you may be doing such a great job that there is a resistance to moving you anywhere at all.

All of this should not be a problem, for a simple reason. When you start the new role, you are hoping to achieve the same success that you have in your current role. And your employer will be expecting this as well. If you take the new role immediately, you will not have had enough time to prepare yourself for success, and therefore your risk of failure will be far higher than it need be. A delay is not a bad thing at all.

To consider this type of change, you will need to speak openly with the person responsible for your career progression. Sometimes this is your manager, but sometimes it may be an HR partner or a generalist in the HR department. And sometimes it is the manager in the target group. Questions you should ask include these:

- What skills are needed to move into this particular position, industry, group, etc.?
- Who else has made a similar move? (You will want to speak directly with those who have made the transition.)
- With the proper preparation, would you see me being successful in this type of role?
- Which partners or senior managers do you suggest I network with?

Once you've developed a relationship with several people within the target group, here are some questions for them:

- What external trade or professional organizations would be helpful for me to join?
- What trade magazines do you regularly review?
- Is there a particular book that helps explain the history and nature of the industry, role, etc.?
- Are there any web sites, blogs, forums, or newsletters that you read on a regular basis?

- Do those in your group have certain professional designations? Do your clients recognize certain designations?

- What are the most important issues and trends on the minds of the clients that you serve? Which issues and trends are new this year?

- And finally, how are new people recruited into the group?

Later, when it's time for you to be interviewed, your preparation will be evident: it's far easier to hire someone who already has the attributes needed for success than someone who just wishes for them.

Several years ago, I was meeting the CEO of a major publishing company to pitch our consulting services to his organization. He asked me many questions, but I believe that two of them were what got my company the job. When answering one of the questions, I mentioned my attendance at BookExpo America, the book industry's annual convention that had taken place a few months earlier. He was surprised that I was there and said so. I responded by saying, "Why wouldn't I be there – that's where everyone in the publishing world is."

His other question was about my view on how to address a new competitive threat. I responded with a comment about the litigation that his parent company had just announced against the newcomer. As soon as I mentioned the litigation (I had read it in the *Wall Street Journal* a few days earlier), he smiled. As far as the CEO was concerned, he was dealing with someone who understood his industry.

If everyone in your target group thinks or acts a particular way, you must learn to model their thinking and their behavior too; not only will it get you the job, it will bring you success once you are there. The flip-side is this: it is unreasonable to expect anyone to offer you a role if you have not begun to model their behavior and thinking.

Staff Rotations

Another option is to change roles, but into a staff job: HR, IT, Accounting, Marketing, as examples. In fact, many departments have rotational positions designed precisely for those who have an interest in the area. Find out if this is the case in your organization and with the target department you are interested in.

One of the more exciting parts of serving clients directly, either in a business development role or a service delivery role, is that your efforts directly affect the client's decisions. If you (and your team) do a great job, you will earn the client's trust, and you will be rewarded by being asked to help address even more critical issues. And of course, you will be rewarded with greater experience, more responsibility, bonuses, and promotion.

When you take on a staff role, your new colleagues will be professionals in their own right, but within the context of your organization, they will likely be viewed "only" as support. While they do have important deadlines, and they do serve internal clients, they generate costs – not revenues. For this reason, there is a very strong focus on cost management (sometimes frustrating), and very little focus on your personal utilization rates (a nice side benefit for you). Despite a reputation to the contrary, most staff professionals work long, long hours. However, in an environment that values utilization and billings, they aren't always recognized for their contribution. Check your ego at the door, and remember that your goal is to learn the staff role and support those who serve the clients directly.

Staff roles can help you understand the business from a new perspective.

There are three primary reasons for considering staff roles:

1. **YOUR LONGER-TERM CAREER GOALS ARE IN THIS AREA.** Or at least you think they are. Taking a staff position will let you develop your budding skills in the area and allow you to test-drive the role. If you like it, you are one step closer to a permanent move into the area. In fact, you may find yourself liking the job so much that you decide to stay in this staff role and seek promotion within your "new" group. If you don't enjoy it, you've just learned a bit more about how the organization works – and you've developed a second network of contacts.

2. **THE SKILLS LEARNED WILL INCREASE YOUR VALUE TO YOUR CLIENTS WHOSE CORE BUSINESSES ARE IN THESE AREAS.** Your ability to understand the client's jargon, key business drivers, and daily pressures will be very different after a period of time working in the same functional area as your clients. Once again, you are using the infrastructure of the firm to help develop skills that are valuable to you and also valuable to the firm's clients.

3. **YOU REALLY DON'T ENJOY YOUR CURRENT JOB, AND YOU WANT TO DO SOMETHING DIFFERENT.** Making this choice does give you an advantage over an external candidate, in the sense that you already understand the structure of the firm, you have an existing network within it, and you have earned a certain degree of credibility. You also understand the client-service side of the business – something that an external hire for the staff role is less likely able to say.

On the other hand, if you are taking a staff role for this last reason, you are effectively running away from something that you don't like – not running to a particular goal you do like. This is not prudent career planning; since you don't have a goal, you will not reach it by following this path. This is the "any port in a storm" strategy. Since there isn't a storm nearby, just dislike of your current job, don't take the easy way out: spend the time determining what your next step should be, using Reality Check Interviews as your guide.

No matter the reason, if you will be considering a move back into former group later, you must address two key issues before accepting the role.

PROFESSIONAL STANDARDS: How long will it take for you to become stale in your area of expertise? Not very long: perhaps as little as three to six months. As you become familiar with your new role, you will be immersed in learning new lingo and new processes; you will have new managers, serve new (internal) clients, and struggle with new deadlines. You will be driven to the same standards of excellence as in your former role, but will have to work twice as hard to achieve it because you don't have the benefit of a background in the area. This effort will leave little time for you to keep up to date in your "former" area of expertise; yet do it you must, otherwise your value doing your old job will have been reduced. Keeping updated means attending the professional development courses for those of your (former) role, and almost more importantly, finding the time to do independent reading and review.

> Stay up-to-date in your primary area of expertise.

REINSERTION: What happens after your two- to three-year commitment into the staff area ends? Depending on your reason for taking the role, you will likely want to move back to your former group. Yet relationships with your clients will have waned, and your place on the team will be taken by other people. Before you accept the staff role, you will want to have assurances that you can go back. From your perspective, you will want this to be an iron-clad guarantee for a specific role, on a specific team, on a specific date. From your employer's perspective, they will tell you to take your chances – no guarantee, no assurance, nothing. Needless to say, many dynamics are at play, and the end result will hopefully be somewhere in the middle.

Several years ago, an established partner transferred into a national firm's senior marketing role for a two-year rotation. Because of the economy, this became a three-year rotation, and then four. Eventually, there was no place for her back on the client service side, and she eventually left. She became the Chief Executive Officer for a large private company – a role that she couldn't have held without the experience earned within the rotational position. Sometimes even the seemingly worst outcomes can turn into tremendous opportunities.

Here are some guidelines to help you in your discussions:

- Make sure that you talk to all concerned about your desire for a time-boxed experience with a reinsertion after that time period. This means your outgoing manager, your prospective incoming manager, and a person in the HR group. The risk to avoid: after your rotation is up, your (then-current) manager is looking to get the next rotational person in, but your former group has no place to put you…

- If you have developed a strong relationship with a senior person (sometimes a mentor, sometimes an official *executive sponsor*), you will be able to call on this person to help ease you back into the appropriate place.

- Ensure that there is a process to discuss your reinsertion: For example, three months before your expected end date, you will speak to persons X and Y; at the same time, you will speak to your then-current manager about your current projects, etc.

- Make sure that you keep your network alive: with your peers, with your managers, and with your staff. They can clue you in to what is happening on the ground while you are "away," and they can ease the transition back later on.

- Consider the possibility of taking on a dual role: during the busy season, you are attached to the client service team, while during less busy time, you report into a staff department.

- Finally, make sure that you understand the impact, if any, on your seniority once you return: will your time away be viewed as a penalty or an advantage?

Non-Traditional Work Arrangements

What would happen if you worked each day only until 3:30 p.m.? Or worked only Monday to Thursday? How would you use your extra time? The list can grow quite a bit, but the alternatives are generally very appealing:

- Spend time with your children when they get home from school
- Care for an elderly parent
- Do gardening and household improvements

- Upgrade your education or training
- Volunteer at your favorite charity
- Take up golf (or some other hobby)
- Train for a marathon
- Take piano or guitar lessons
- Just relax

On the other hand, because you will be working fewer hours each period, the trade-off is that you will not be gaining experience at the same rate as if you had a full, traditional workload. The impact of this will be felt in two ways. It may take you longer to earn promotions, and because of lower visibility, the strength of your internal relationships may also suffer.

Working a reduced work week can happen in a number of different ways:

JOB SHARING: This arrangement shares one set of responsibilities between two people. This can be of the "You-work-mornings-I-work-afternoons" variety, or "You-work-Monday-Tuesday-I-work-the-rest." It is easiest if responsibilities are completely divided, so that the job-sharing pair would not need to coordinate hand-offs. To be successful when responsibilities aren't divided, hand-offs need to be coordinated, and there needs to be a strong degree of trust between the job-sharing pair. The challenge with job sharing is that you need to identify someone else who seeks the same type of arrangement, who also has similar skills and capabilities.

FLEX-TIME: Instead of a standard 9-to-5 job (or 8-to-8 job?), under flex-time you are given the flexibility to do the tasks on your timing, so long as you meet certain minimum conditions. These may be that you be in the office (or at the client site) during certain core hours each day, or during certain core days each week. Otherwise, you are free to work your allotted hours on the weekends, the very, very early morning, the evenings, or some other combination. The major benefits of flex-time are that it allows recapture of time wasted during rush hour and it allows alternative child-care arrangements. In my case, it allows me to be at home when my youngest daughter comes home from school. Usually, a flex-time arrangement can be suspended during peak busy periods.

COMPRESSED WORK WEEK: Instead of doing your work over five days, why not over a lesser number? Most mature managers recognize that their staff are being paid to complete a task – not show up at a job. So long as you complete the task at a professional level, by the appropriate deadline, then whether you do the work over five, four, or three days should not really make a difference. Of course, if you do the work over fewer days, those days will be much longer – but the total number of working hours should remain the same.

One big advantage of a compressed work week is that less of your time is spent doing unproductive activities – like travel. Another is that you can schedule time for other Personal Balance Sheet activities (community work, intellectual growth, family, fitness, etc.) on a more regular basis.

A reduced work-week may require flexibility and compromise.

If you are interested in a compressed work week, recognize that certain constraints may require flexibility on your part. For example, clients may expect to see you "on site" every day, and you may have difficulty helping them understand your working hours. Or there may be requirements in your own organization for you to attend training or critical meetings on non-scheduled days.

REDUCED WORKLOAD: Sometimes referred to as *full-time part-time*, this arrangement essentially means cutting your working hours – and therefore your pay – each week.

Before you discard this alternative as one that is impossible financially, first determine how much the cut would actually cost. Most progressive employers won't cut your benefits, unless your "full-time" weekly hours go below a set floor – often 25 or 30 hours.

If you reduce to an 80% schedule, it is your gross pay that is cut, not your net. After tax, depending on your tax bracket, your net pay might not take as much of a hit as you think. Furthermore, if you get a car as a benefit, you may be able to negotiate for a less expensive car (or at least the same model with fewer options), but more salary.

Here are some ideas to help you negotiate this type of arrangement:

- Ensure that you have a plan as to how the rest of your responsibilities will be handled. This will likely be the biggest issue you will have to address.

- Redefine job objectives and goals to account for your different schedule.

- Indicate your flexibility: if a meeting can be held only at a time when you are not in the office, you will make every effort to attend.

- Find others in the organization who have successfully been able to negotiate a reduced work schedule; ask them about their experience both negotiating the arrangement and living it.

- Build in a meeting one month into the new arrangement to discuss how it is proceeding. If there are problems, it's best to formally address them while they're still small.

One of my clients relates an interesting story. Upon return from maternity leave several years ago, she found herself with a new manager. When my client was asked by her new manager what she was looking for in her job, she told him, and also mentioned in passing that a four-day work week would be desirable. A few weeks later, he called her into his office and told her that a four-day week was possible, if she was interested. Years (and a significant promotion) later, she is still working a reduced work schedule successfully. While her manager was quite exceptional (and still is), this story illustrates well the adage "If you don't ask, you don't get!"

The major risk in this kind of arrangement is one that increases as one rises in seniority. As a junior manager, job sharing, reduced workloads, and short-term leaves are relatively easy to manage, as others typically will fill in while you are not there. As you become more senior, though, the company demands your nights, weekends, breakfast, lunch, and dinner. You are expected to run at 120% in order to meet your agreed-upon objectives. Because of this, there are few who can fill in for you while you're not around. The more senior you get, the more likely you'll find yourself being paid 80% *for the same 120% commitment*!

> Don't find yourself being paid 80% for the same 120% commitment.

If you are able to address these issues, you will still need to manage your colleagues' perceptions. To avoid paying a political price, you will need to help those around you understand your time boundaries.

Sabbaticals

CASE ONE: For whatever reason, you may have it in your mind to quit. Not a problem – you're not only an adult, but also a professional who has earned the right to make your own career decisions.

CASE TWO: You and your family are considering a three-month sailing trip around the world, and you only have four weeks' vacation.

CASE THREE: You have been taking a part-time MBA for a number of years, and a short-term switch to the full-time program will let you finish it quickly.

Whichever the case, you may see quitting as the only alternative – but there is another. After all, why throw away all of your hard-won credibility (and seniority)?

What if you approached your employer and asked for an extended (unpaid) leave? You might find that your employer has leave policies already in place that you can tap into. And in some cases, you may still be eligible to receive employee benefits.

Here are some basic guidelines for asking for an extended leave:

1. **There should be no surprises:** Make sure that you speak to your manager with enough notice, and at a time when their attention can be fully focused on your discussion.

2. **The timing must work for both parties, not just you:** If you are hoping to take a sabbatical over the busiest time of the year, it is unlikely that your request will be granted.

3. **Ensure coverage:** who will do your job while you're away? Come up with two alternatives, and be prepared to present your ideas during the conversation. This will likely be your employer's biggest issue. Thankfully, most managers have experience planning through maternity (and paternity) leaves.

4. **Look around for others who have taken a leave:** How did they ask? What issues cropped up during their absence and upon their return? How did they deal with those issues?

5. **Consider your return:** Review the section above on Staff Rotations – some of it is equally applicable here. There is a related issue, however, that may give you pause: they may not want you back! Your employer may feel that if they can do without you for three months, maybe they don't need you at all! Or they backfill your position with someone more to their liking and decide that this new person should stay in the job.

In Chapter 24, extended leaves are explored in greater detail.

Join a Client

One of the touchier areas of career change is when an employee joins a client.

Those who see it as an ethical or legal issue use the terms *poaching* and *solicitation* to describe it. They are concerned about two things: they are losing an excellent employee (you), and they may be losing the value that you generate. After all, so the reasoning goes, it's cheaper for the client to have an employee do the job than outsource it.

On the other hand, there will be another group that is pleased you've found a friendly new home. Since your knowledge about the firm is so good, when you need help, you will call on your friends, which will yield increased billings and more special projects. Furthermore, since you have that affinity, you are far less likely to move business to a competitor. Most organizations recognize your external value and have set up strong alumni programs, specifically designed to strengthen your commitment after you have left.

One of the interesting dynamics if you were to become the client: your boss, and possibly your boss's boss, will likely both be serving you. This reversal of roles can result in an interesting dynamic. When they managed you, they did their best given their personal abilities. When you manage them, you should do your best given your personal abilities. Whether you are on the client service side or the client side, maintaining a professional relationship should be your primary goal.

Understand your employer's guidelines regarding a move to a client or supplier.

A former colleague of mine was constantly – and unfairly – put under the gun by the manager in charge of the group. He was given the least interesting assignments, was given little admin support, and was excluded from certain group activities. Despite this, he did excellent work, helped his other (junior) colleagues without hesitation, and continued to earn promotions, albeit at a slower pace. Many years later, he had left the firm to be the head of a pension plan client, and his nemesis had left to be the head of an organization that was funded… by that very same pension plan. The roles were reversed. Was it payback time – or was there a professional relationship? What would you do?

While there might be great personal satisfaction in squeezing a former manager, our business environment is very, very small; it would not be unreasonable to expect that the roles might be reversed yet again, sometime in the future. Managing your relationships professionally to the best of your ability should be your primary goal.

Many organizations have very strict guidelines on the process that you should go through if you wish to work for a client. The guidelines might exist for professional reasons: to ensure independence and objectivity while an interview process is ongoing, as an example. The guidelines might exist for succession planning or client service continuity reasons. In fact, depending on your employment contract, standards of practice, conflict of interest guidelines, and other standards of employment, you may find that you are precluded from being hired by specific clients. And certain clients may be precluded from hiring you completely or precluded from hiring you without paying substantial additional fees to your employer.

You should be concerned about two issues. The first is whether these restrictions that you have explicitly and implicitly agreed to have a legal basis or not; the second is the ethics (and optics) of you contravening them. Remember to consider the perspective of the person who is giving you advice. If a recruiter tells you that there is no issue, they may be telling you the truth, or they may be unduly influenced by their 25 to 35% commission riding on your departure! If a lawyer tells you that you are within your rights to move if you so choose, remember that they are speaking only of your legal rights, not the ethics of it. As well, neither recruiters nor lawyers are concerned with your longer-term relationships in our small-world business environment: usually their concerns are primarily transactional. A trusted mentor or an experienced career coach who understands the industry may be able to provide more objective guidance. Whether you go or stay, remember that it is your relationships that have the value.

Legal rights and ethics are not necessarily the same.

Move to Government, Regulator, Institute, Association, etc.

With so much experience in your industry, you may have generated a public profile within it. Taking your *brand equity* and moving to an organization that either speaks for your industry or regulates it is an interesting way for you to leverage your knowledge – while providing you with a different intellectual spin.

This type of move could also be of interest if you are looking to combine your professional expertise with a personal interest: health care, seniors, or a faith community, as examples. In fact, the sophistication in the charitable sector rivals that of many businesses.

You will have to feel comfortable with a number of changes if you make this type of move, most having to do with the differences between the for-profit and the not-for-profit dimension of the organization.

Depending on the role that you are seeking, some of your experience will be transferable, and some will not. For example, people who fundraise play an important role within not-for-profit organizations. Yet does this role have an analog in the for-profit world? The answer is "Somewhat": sales executives, for example, have some of the required experience. But most sales executives are used to selling a tangible product, not a less tangible set of goals. If your skills are in marketing, finance, or operations, these skills might be a bit more transferable, but what is your experience dealing with minuscule marketing budgets? How about volunteers instead of employees? And financial systems that aren't quite as up to date as you're used to?

NON-FINANCIAL OBJECTIVES ARE PRIMARY: You're likely used to a system that pressures for higher sales with lower costs. But are you prepared for organizational performance being ranked primarily by non-financial objectives? Would you remain personally motivated without a traditional financial scorecard? On the ground, this may mean less focus on utilization, and greater focus on less measurable projects.

STAKEHOLDER DIFFERENCES: In the corporate setting, the number one stakeholder groups are usually considered to be the clients, then variously owners, employees, the community, and if applicable, regulators. We tend to value "focus," spend most of our time with one or two of these groups, and keep the rest on maintenance mode. In a not-for-profit, the weightings are skewed differently, often with the community, media, regulators, and special interest groups nearing the very top of the list and having real weight.

SENSE OF URGENCY: Most organizations understand the importance of speed, from the impact of a faster product development cycle on costs, to the impact that faster client service has on client retention. The Internet, and all the expectations it has engendered, has heightened pressure for speed even further. In many non-profits (and many areas of government), a sense of urgency just does not exist, as the incentive for speed is not as great as in the private sector. And in some organizations, attributes such as speed rank far behind other attributes, such as equity, need, or public accountability. That being said, many not-for-profit organizations are exceptionally well-managed, and their sense of urgency is second to none.

Consider a volunteer board role in the not-for-profit sector prior to a permanent move.

PERSONNEL POLICIES: Staff retention and longevity are usually very high for non-profits, regulators, and associations, often because the jobs tend not to be as pressured as corporate jobs are. Unfortunately, in some non-profits, retention is high because there are often poor (or non-existent) personnel policies and practices.

Many non-profits use volunteers at every level: for governance, as advisors, within committees, and as arms-and-legs at events. This adds a complication: your management style must properly motivate them to action. If you need to fire or discipline them, the mechanism to do so is different yet again. And in certain organizations (usually governmental), there is also the issue of managing within a unionized environment.

If you decide that this isn't the career option for you, but you are still interested in the sector, consider the many volunteer leadership opportunities, either at the board level or through membership on the various committees.

Boomerang/Returnee

If you liked an earlier employer and are not sure whether your longer-term career should remain where you currently reside, what is stopping you from returning to that earlier employer – becoming a returnee?

Often it is ego: you may have a certain fear that you are returning because you have "failed" outside. And for some people, you left because you failed "inside." Even if you did in fact "fail" inside, you have since gained a tremendous amount of new experience, and you have developed into a far more mature manager. As we have discussed earlier, the reasons for leaving an employer are exceptionally wide. The stigma of "failure" is likely stronger in your mind than anywhere else; banish the thoughts, and let your accomplishments speak for themselves.

If you liked your former employer before, you probably still do.

After you have spent a number of years outside, you will have learned many things, including the following:

- The grass isn't always greener on the other side of the fence. Said another way, you may not have seen as intense a challenge as you had expected.

- You will have worn the shoes of the clients and now understand intimately their issues and daily pressures.

- You now know an industry as someone who lives in it. And your reputation (and network) within it has expanded as a result.

- Your relationships with your former employer may now be at a far more senior level.

- You will have deepened relationships in the community, providing for later business development opportunities.

- At the same time, you will have a few extra bruises earned through your new experiences.

The question from your former (and now prospective) employer's point of view is simple: what isn't there to like about the *new you*? If you go back, they will likely see you as someone who is committed for the long term. You've already tasted the outside and have made the positive decision to come back home.

If you do end up leaving your current employer, remember to keep the boomerang option open: don't burn bridges on the way out. And keep your relationships alive when you're gone – you never know what will happen.

Start-Up/Entrepreneur

Becoming an entrepreneur is one of the most challenging alternatives, but it can also be quite satisfying when success finally comes. You will be competing against established organizations that have customer relationships, supplier deals in place, brand equity, and likely a stronger financial base. However, your start-up might not have the overheads or the "old technology" that constrain your entrenched competitors. Your new perspective and out-of-the-box thinking might be able to change the rules of the game, giving you a sustainable competitive advantage.

A start-up is special from another perspective as well. Everything is new. There are no established processes, policies, or procedures. There are no "HR departments," succession-planning issues, or 25-year long-service awards. While you may enjoy the title of president or managing partner, unwittingly you will also have the title of janitor, secretary, messenger, purchasing clerk, IT wizard, and anything else that is not directly someone else's responsibility. Developing a start-up operation is sometimes described as giving birth to a vision.

Is there a way to "test-drive" the business beforehand?

If the business is in an area that is not known to you, what can be done to reduce your risks? And is there a way for you to "test-drive" the business beforehand? Sometimes, the answer is *yes*. Certainly you can interview people who have done what you're proposing, but to really understand the business means having the courage to *live* the business for a period of time. If you have decided to open a restaurant, would you be willing to work part-time evenings or weekends as a dishwasher or busboy?

Entrepreneurial Start-Up (With and Without Partners)

Although you may be tempted to open up your business by yourself, going into a partnership has some advantages. Start-up financing may be easier. You can share the management load (hopefully). There is always someone who will have the same loyalty and drive as you (hopefully). You will each bring complementary skills (hopefully). And so on.

The risks in a partnership have to do with the word "hopefully." Nobody enters into a marriage with the expectation of divorce. But unless responsibilities and expectations are fully agreed to, and then "lived" on a

Make sure that you have a signed partnership agreement. daily basis by all partners, it is likely that the partnership will fall apart. And when that happens, the value of the business usually drops precipitously.

If you are going into a partnership, make absolutely sure that you have a written partnership agreement that includes, at least, a separation, dissolution, or buy-out clause.[3] What else should be in the agreement? Division of responsibilities, determination of compensation, ownership structure, and ownership of client relationships, along with the answers to many "what-ifs." If you invest in nothing else, you and your partner(s) should spend money getting an appropriate legal agreement drafted.

Competing with Your Former Employer

Starting a business that is in competition with a former employer bears special mention and should be done with caution. Certainly as a professional advisor, the only thing that has value is your reputation. If you will be competing against your firm, make sure that you follow all due process to ensure you will not be accused of stealing clients or employees. If there is a perception of either of these, you may be compromising your reputation – and opening yourself to a lawsuit. And with your mind on expensive legal actions, it will not be on growing your business or serving your clients. More than anything else, your reputation is the most valuable asset you have – once it goes, you will not have a business.

Some major firms have established processes to ensure that anyone who exits to start up as a competitor does so under particular terms.

One of the things that you might notice is that your organization may no longer be capable of delivering a certain type of work. Or they have made a decision to de-emphasize a certain type of business, yet you still see a great opportunity in the area. In both of these cases, there may be interest on the part of your organization to sell you that block of business. I know of no firm, though, that would gladly give up clients. If you are hoping to hang out your own shingle, expect to earn your clients the hard way – one by one.

---

3   One form of this is the so-called shotgun clause. If partner A wishes to buy out partner B at a specific price, B can turn around and require A to sell the business to B at that specific price.

Consultancy/Free Agent

One of the major differences between consulting (anywhere) and most other jobs is that each engagement must be individually sold and delivered. Once completed, that's it; it would be rare for the engagement to be repeated on an annual basis. For this reason, business development skills are as important as service delivery skills.

Typical professional services organizations will price their resources somewhere between $100 and $500 or even more per hour. For that fee, the client gets a number of things: the "guarantee" behind the work, a proven methodology, no training expenses, no HR administration costs, and sundry other benefits. Clients would also get top-notch staff who know their subject intimately and can thus add value well beyond their cost.

The economics of the industry, however, require that a partner be used to sell the job, and a manager and a few juniors would deliver. The partner's special expertise would address only the more sophisticated aspects of the engagement, and if it starts to fall off the rails, they would jump in and put it right.

Becoming a free agent takes this model and turns it around. Your clients will get a top-flight advisor – you – who has the experience to solve their very pressing problems. Compared to industry-outsider consultants who come up with recommendations and then leave, you have "felt the pain" and have the experience to solve problems realistically and pragmatically. Likely, your clients will expect to pay much less for your services than for the name-brand firms; this shouldn't be a problem for you: your overheads are far lower, and your net after-tax earnings will likely be higher as you can write off a number of previously non-deductible expenses (such as home office).

Hiring an independent consultant, which you may have done before, is very different from being one. Unique stresses come with this type of work. Your time must be split between selling and delivering your services, two very different skill sets. Whenever you are not working (for example, when you are on vacation, when you are selling, or when you are in training), you do not get paid. And you must realize that your big, corporately grown ego must be shunted aside, as consultants get all the blame when things go wrong and none of the credit when things are successful. Another major change will be that of handling the billings and receivables. You learn to appreciate the "magic" of having your pay deposited automatically each month only when this no longer happens!

Many years ago, I did significant work for a client during the first 15 days of the month, and then, per our agreement, billed at the end of the month. They received the invoice at the beginning of the next month, put it in a 30-day "hold queue," and then paid it on the next payment cycle – the end of that month. I received my payment a week later. Effectively, I was the Bank of Randall Craig for three months! Worse, I had incurred out-of-pocket expenses on their behalf, so my business was not only financing time, but their expenses! For a quarter of the year! As a free agent, one learns very quickly about the difference between "It's in the mail" and having the money in your hand!

Being a consultant is very different than hiring one.

However, if you are the type of person who continually enjoys diving into the deep end, gets immense satisfaction from saying "I did that" (even if nobody else knows), and enjoys working with strong management teams in different organizations, then consulting is worth a try.

To test-drive consulting is not so easy, because the sell-cycle for any specific engagement is either too long, there is a time conflict with your current position (can't be in two places at once), or there is a business conflict with your current employer. To understand the business of consulting, consider talking to the independent consultants you know, and read a few books on the subject. Two great books on the subject are *Managing the Professional Services Firm* and *The Trusted Advisor*, both by David Maister.

Another option, if consulting interests you, is to get a job in the consulting division of your organization.

Your challenge may be your inexperience: you may lack the specialized skills required to deliver a typical engagement. As a result, you may be required to move "down" a level, putting in your time to learn the firm's methodologies and hone new skills. Another way to accomplish this goal is to work on jointly delivered projects. In both cases, you will need to begin developing relationships with the managers in charge of the groups you are interested in.

If you are hoping to get slotted in at a manager/senior manager level, mid-tier hires must usually have a unique quality to be considered:

- Strong enough business development skills to achieve a high margin beyond your salary.
- Special knowledge that can be exploited firm-wide (e.g., if you helped draft specific legislation, or if you have an obscure technical skill).

- Unique relationships that can be exploited firm-wide. (Usually these are exploited either for business development or lobbying purposes.)

If you do get hired under these circumstances, remember that your value generally ends when your unique quality is no longer unique. If this is your entry strategy, you must work doubly hard to parlay your job into something else relatively quickly, or keep your special knowledge well on the leading edge. Otherwise, when your value ends, so will your job.

Purchase an Existing Business

The major benefit of purchasing a business is that everything doesn't have to be started from scratch. Processes exist, people exist, systems exist; relationships with customers, suppliers, and the bank are usually long-standing, if not strong.

If you are purchasing a smaller enterprise, the biggest risk is that the customers will leave when the owner/manager does. The second-biggest risk is that you are not able to successfully do the knowledge transfer from the outgoing owner/manager. If you are purchasing a medium or larger enterprise, the biggest risks usually revolve around the unfound skeletons in the closet and the quality of the management team. Even if you consider yourself an expert in the area, if you are looking to purchase a business, get professional help both for the negotiations and the due diligence. Thoughtfully consider what you learn from the due diligence prior to moving forward with any transaction.

It would be impossible to do justice to this alternative in a few pages; indeed, entire books have been written on the subject. Instead, we'll review four different purchase strategies: franchises, successions, structural change, and avocation.

Franchise Purchase

The benefit of running a franchise is that most of the thinking is already done for you. For your franchise fee (and many, many obligations under the franchise agreement), you slot yourself in, follow the manual, and operate. Usually, the franchise owner is on the front line themselves, often as much to reduce costs as to provide the management function.

For many readers of this book, franchise ownership may not be a fit. Of course, for some, "following the manual" is appealing, and for them, a particular franchise might be just the right thing. If you are interested, visit the franchise trade shows in your area, and check bookstores for franchise guides.

A more proactive variation on this theme would be the purchase of a master franchise for your country or region. Essentially, you would license the name, operating manuals, and processes of a successful foreign franchise organization, make appropriate changes for your market, and become the franchisor within your territory. Master franchise agreements are a mechanism for the foreign franchisor to both earn "today income" and open new geographic regions, without committing capital or consuming management time.

To find a suitable master franchise candidate, consider spending time at foreign franchise trade shows. Less productive, but perhaps more fun, is to look for concepts as you do your personal travel abroad.

Succession Purchase

Especially in family-run businesses, succession planning is either neglected or not done as rigorously as it should be. By the time the majority owner is ready for retirement, internal (or family) leadership candidates are often long gone or uninterested. When there is no heir apparent, and the uninvolved family ownership group is looking to cash out, there may be an opportunity to make an unsolicited offer.

The biggest risk is if key employees quit just after your purchase.

If you do purchase this type of company, be prepared to deal with nepotism, as well as the effects of low infrastructure or technology investment. Recently, a medical professional friend discovered this the hard way. After purchasing several diagnostic clinics, he kept all of the employees, including two of the previous owner's adult children. His rationale was that it would be good for business continuity and knowledge transfer. He quickly discovered that they added little to the business and had to fire them – with a costly exit package. When their replacements were hired, he only then discovered the extent of the problems with the technology. Of course, *caveat emptor* in any purchase, but when family is involved, it is just that much more complex.

Structural Change Purchase

An industry structure may change for a variety of reasons: changing technology, new channel entrants, mergers and acquisitions, vertical integration, changes in regulatory or political environments, just to name a few. If you believe that a particular industry will not look the same in the future as it does now, you should consider purchasing a company that can be positioned to take advantage of that change.

Needless to say, the risks here are that your analysis is off, and the industry structure does change, but not exactly as you imagined it to. Mitigate your risk by testing out different change scenarios during the acquisition process, and then plan for those contingencies. Spend time reading all the industry reports, interviewing industry analysts, and attending industry conferences. These activities can identify potential candidates – and mitigate risk further.

Avocation Purchase

Business success is determined by both inspiration and perspiration. Perspiration is easy – most successful managers do this quite well, but where does the inspiration come from? Purchasing a business in an area of great personal interest makes inspiration easy.

A risk, however, is that your personal subjectivity and ego get in the way of your business judgment of the merits of the opportunity.

You are far more likely to be successful when you have passion for your business.

A colleague in my martial arts club, a Black Belt, was a long-time salesman for industrial parts in the telecommunications sector. He had been training in karate for many years in a large city and after being transferred back to his home town started to teach karate part-time to maintain his own training. A number of years later, he was still teaching karate and enjoying it. His day job, on the other hand, was stressful and uncertain: he didn't enjoy it at all. As sometimes happens, fate intervenes; in his case, a retail martial arts supply store was put up for sale. He took it and hasn't looked back since.

Let's consider his risks: he had no experience in retail, let alone how to run his own business. He also didn't have a plan beforehand. He didn't take any small business management courses, nor did he have a chance to test-drive a retail working experience. But what he lacked in knowledge, he more than made up with inspiration and perspiration. When the opportunity presented itself, he grabbed it.

Generally the way to find acquisition candidates (whether they be successions, structural change, or avocation purchases) is to work your network. Tell your lawyer, accountant, bank manager, and insurance agent your acquisition criteria; they are well positioned to know of any potential opportunities.

Trading Up: Working at Another Large Organization

This is certainly the most traditional external next step. You are the CFO of a $25-million company and seek a position as the CFO of a $50-million company. You are a manager with a portfolio of 15 products, and you seek a position with a portfolio of 25 or more. Or you are a specialist in a mid-sized organization and are looking for greater challenges.

The most important reason that trading up is such an attractive option is that you will likely stay in the same, or similar, industry. You can keep and leverage both your knowledge and your contact base. You love what you do, but are looking for greater challenge on a higher scale.

Be prepared for a reaction if you are moving to a competitor. Depending on whether you are constrained by non-compete agreements, there may be some further negotiations. And separately, if it is a direct competitor, you may be asked to leave immediately.

If you are working as an accountant or lawyer, you may be considering a move into the financial services world. There is no question that with your credentials you will have a leg up on those without. But recognize that there is a fundamental difference between working in a corporate environment and a partnership one. In a partnership you are working directly for the owners of the organization. In a larger corporation, you aren't: the owners are disconnected from the day-to-day decisions of the organization. Even in smaller corporations, the hierarchy and decision-making are different. This difference reverberates into every corner of the business.

Trading Down: Working at a Smaller Organization

Like moving to a larger company, moving to a smaller company is also a conventional alternative. Many years ago, I decided to sell my beautiful BMW 5-series car and replace it with a tiny (and not particularly attractive) Suzuki Swift. I loved driving the BMW, but I didn't really need it and was looking to spend the money on other priorities at the time. When you make this type of a change – whether a car, house, or job – you must be prepared for it. The Suzuki didn't accelerate like the BMW, nor did it have power leather seats. The Suzuki dealer service wasn't up to the standards of BMW either. But it sure was cheap to fill up the tank! If you move to a smaller organization, be prepared for a few surprises of your own (both positive and negative), and go with the flow; it's a lot less stressful.

Why move to a smaller organization in the first place? This type of move is usually made for one of two reasons. Maybe you are looking for an increased scope of responsibility, or maybe for a new management challenge, such as a turnaround. Or maybe you've just had too much of the rat race and are looking for a less stressful environment.

Increased Scope

Consider a person who is at the top of their functional ladder, but has made their mark in an organization that does not "cross-promote" into general management. (For example, a CFO who works in a company that takes the president from the marketing or sales side of the business.) One way for this person to become a company head is to accept the role of president in a smaller organization, prove themselves, and then trade up. While this may seem like a one-step-backwards for two-steps-forward approach, it gives you several benefits:

- The ability to learn the job in another organization. Don't forget, you may have had senior experience with only one company so far; developing general management skills elsewhere will help you cultivate a more flexible management style. This will pay off in the long run.

- Because you have already been (in the above example) a CFO for a larger company, you bring greater credibility in this area than a leader without the experience. As this area will be less of a risk for you, your full attention can be focused on learning how to fill the new role.

Turnaround (Or Other Management Challenge)

Smaller companies often have challenges that their bigger competitors have already met. These challenges can be financial (avoiding bankruptcy, going public), managing growth, or perhaps solving a particular operational problem. The company has determined that the best course of action is to recruit externally. They are looking for a candidate who can say, "Been there, done that," and then actually get it done.

Why would you want to consider this type of situation? Again, it may be for the personal challenge and managerial growth, but another reason may be more practical. As part of your compensation, your package will likely include an equity component, and your upside may be quite high.

Of course, the downside is that if you are not successful in your objectives, you have a black mark on your resumé that you will eventually have to justify. This shouldn't preclude you from looking at turn-around situations, if that is what excites you: the risk of a "black mark" exists no matter what you choose to do.

"Too Much"

The organization that you have grown up with has likely matured too, and with that growth have come changes. Some of the changes (increased scope, promotions, authority, etc.) may have been positive, but some may not be to your liking. For example, you may be spending too much time travelling away from your family. Or you may have to spend several evenings each week at business functions.

For whatever reason, moving to a smaller organization may help solve some of these problems, if you make your choice properly.

Here's a different perspective: as organizations grow, they need different types of managers; by moving to a smaller organization, you are pre-emptively aligning your skills (and comfort) with that new organization.

If you haven't been to a job interview for a few years, you should keep this fact in mind: you're interviewing the company as much as they're interviewing you. In the end, they are looking to buy your professional experience, as much as you're looking to sell it.

You are interviewing the company as much as they are interviewing you.

Earn a Graduate Degree or Professional Certification (Full or Part-Time)

Any port in a storm is the strategy that is often used by the newly laid-off to justify the pursuit of an advanced education. While not very strategic, an educational pursuit is a rationale that can be easily explained to prospective employers when the job search begins yet again, in earnest.

Deciding to pursue full-time studies means a substantial financial sacrifice, often for two years or more. Despite these financial consequences, there may be some important reasons for doing so anyway:

- **GLASS CEILING ISSUE:** If you are a treasurer looking to become a CFO, you might find fewer opportunities unless you have an MBA. You may be a teacher looking to move into curriculum design; yet without an M.Ed., you might never be considered for the position.

- **DESIRE FOR CAREER SHIFT:** After many years climbing through a functional silo, you understand many of the related jobs, but need a formal education for qualification. Examples include an accountant who decides to specialize in financial planning, an insurance underwriter who decides to become an actuary, or a nurse who wishes to become a physical therapist.

- **CHANGED BUSINESS ENVIRONMENT:** Since your graduation, the business environment may have changed substantially. Legislation, Technologies, and Research in your field are but a few of the things that are new. An educational investment will update your value, and help you communicate with clients and colleagues about the impact of change.

- **PERSONAL NEED FOR INTELLECTUAL CHALLENGE:** You may feel that you haven't been using your "head" much during the last number of years, and that doing intensive study for several years will give you an intellectual jump-start. Review your Job Quality Checklist results. How did you answer the question about appropriate intellectual challenge?

- **ACADEMIC CAREER ENTRY POINT:** Pretty much the only way to become a college or university professor is to earn a PhD. These typically must be done on a full-time basis.

You may be in a position where your employer provides matching donations to non-profit institutions, including colleges and universities. If the normal annual tuition was $20,000, perhaps you could arrange to make a "donation" of $12,000 (in lieu of normal tuition), which was then matched dollar-for-dollar by your employer. The college does better by $4,000, as do you, by $8,000.

MBA options include full-time, part-time, online, executive, and international.

If you are in a more senior role, your organization may provide funding (full or partial) for an Executive MBA (EMBA). In this case, classes are typically held on weekends or sometimes alternate Fridays. EMBA students are typically a bit older, and given that you learn as much from your classmates as from your professors, the value of the EMBA is commensurately greater.

Spend time reviewing the scholarships and grants that are available, both from public and private sources. Many large reference libraries, bookstores, and web sites have entire sections devoted to this subject. And some of the awards are significant.

It is also worthwhile exploring the options for pursuing advanced education on a part-time basis. While it may take longer to complete your studies, you will not suffer the financial consequences of zero income nor have the immediate post-graduation uncertainty of finding another position. Your current employer may even cover some or all of your costs. This option can be appealing if it provides exactly what is missing from your current workplace: intellectual challenge.

There is no reason you cannot apply the same analytical rigor to the MBA decision that you apply to a work-day business decision. Before committing to an advanced degree (whether full-time or part-time), do an ROI analysis: will the benefits outweigh the costs? Putting aside for a moment the human element, what compensation changes will an MBA bring, both immediately and over the medium or long term? And what is the investment required to earn that return? Here are a few questions that can help:

- Does your employer have a tuition reimbursement policy? Will it pay for textbooks and other non-tuition costs?

- Will your employer pay a bonus (or adjust your salary) upon completion?

- Will your level, or your eligibility for promotion, change as a result of completing the degree?

- Will an MBA open an alternative career path that provides a higher level of compensation?

- By concentrating on an MBA, will you be forgoing options for advancement, or any other income-earning opportunities?

- If you will be incurring debt to pay for the degree, what will this debt cost be?

- Is there an opportunity cost to not having this degree? Will certain positions be forever closed to you without one?

Doing an MBA requires family and workplace support.

After you calculate the notional ROI on a strictly numbers basis, you can then layer on the emotional and relationship costs, and the emotional and relationship benefits, to determine whether it is worthwhile doing.

Finally, don't underestimate the cost that a heavy workload imposes on personal relationships, especially with a part-time course of studies. Indeed, an expression that is often repeated among new part-time MBA students is "Job, Family, MBA: choose two." If you "choose three," make sure the choice is one that is understood by all parties concerned: you, your family, and your workplace. Otherwise, you may learn of the other popular name for the MBA: the divorce course.

"Volunteer" and Community Service Work as a Full-Time Vocation

Very few people have the financial independence to quit paid work and donate their time 100% to the community, but if you can, why not consider it? Often, there is a dearth of strong leaders and managers in community service work, precisely because the best are often looking to establish the financial independence you already have.

If a full-time donation is impossible, spending some of your time doing volunteer work can still pay off. The return on your time investment certainly will be in personal satisfaction, but it can also be in strong relationships with other senior people in the community.

Stay at Home with Kids or Parents

Today, many young professionals are feeling the pressure of being the sandwich generation: it is no longer just younger children, but older parents who require (sometimes daily) mindshare. Deciding to spend time with your loved ones exactly when they need it can give a personal satisfaction well beyond any money that the next step in your career can provide.

Many people today feel that staying at home to be a full-time care-giver is not a financially viable option. While this concern is true for some, if you have the will, you can often find a way. (And if you have special needs children or acutely ill parents, you may not have a choice.)

You may feel stigmatized with the title "househusband" or "housewife." Just remember the reason you're doing it – your children (or your parents) will never fault you for spending too much time with them. This might not hold as true for teenage children, but that is another issue.

If you decide to be a full-time caregiver, you will likely miss the stimulation and challenge of the working world. Consider taking on the occasional consulting assignment to keep sharp, and increasing your community involvement to take up the slack. Enrolling in formal courses will help both keep you up-to-date in your area of expertise, and avoid some of the feelings of isolation and loneliness. As well, if there is a seasonal busy time (tax season, year-ends, etc), a seasonal commitment to your career might give you the best of both worlds.

While plans often change, decide on a timeframe after which you will return to the workforce – whether it be three months, two years, or until a particular milestone. This will help structure your time, and give you a better "story" to tell upon your return.

Do Something Non-traditional

If your career has been in the corporate world, some decidedly non-corporate job choices might be to become a writer, work in a developing country, or become an interior designer. But if you come from a family of writers, or if you were born in a developing country, these "non-traditional" work choices are actually quite traditional. In fact, the concept of "non-traditional" itself is a relative term. Perhaps all it really means is that it is a choice that you (and others among your peers and family) hadn't considered.

There is really no limit to the possibilities of how you can spend your time. Yet if you have a strong desire for a specific non-traditional job choice, you should make sure you understand what that job is all about. Sometimes we will romanticize our "crazy" ideas so much that no matter what type of success we currently have, we become cynical and resentful of our current situation. And sometimes resentful of our friends and families.

Others may not understand your non-traditional choice.

And when we announce our new job and career, those around us (who should be supporting us, after all) instead ask us nosy questions, supposedly for our own good. They question our decisions. They ask how we can throw away all that we have accomplished. This creates a spiral where we do not want their support... which is exactly what we will need to succeed in the new role!

Remember that people assume you are driven by the same forces that drive them; they don't understand how your decision could possibly make sense. Other reactions are from people close to you, where there is a concern about how a change will affect them. And others will have a genuine concern about whether you are making the right decision. In all these cases, helping them understand how and why you came to your decisions will help reduce their stress, and yours.

To do this, you have to make sure that you know the answers for yourself – and that you are not succumbing to the allure of a romantic ideal. This can be done in several ways:

Job research and networking: What are the key success factors for those considering this type of position?

Test drive: Is there a way to try out the non-traditional job, so that you can get a first-hand feel for it? If not, can you at least get a part-time or volunteer job in a related field?

Fill in the gaps: What preparation do you need to do between now and when you start the role, to improve the chances of your success?

Answer the *what's next* question: Assuming that you move into the role, after two or three years, what would the next step be?

Review the Job Quality Checklist and your Personal Balance Sheet: When communicating with others, these frameworks provide evidence that your decision was a thoughtful, considered one.

Your goal should be to engage your support networks more meaningfully, and at the same time improve your chances of success in the role itself.

⟫◆⟪

Triggering Events

When the ball drops. The expression itself got its start in New York's Times Square: when the ball dropped, it was the end of the old year, and the beginning of the new one.

Many times throughout our lives we have similar epiphanies; something happens, and we figuratively wake up with a new realization.

In a certain sense, the purpose of this book is to hasten this process for you. Too often, the career ball drops, and we are unprepared to make the right decisions. Recognizing different triggering events before they happen can reduce our surprise for when they do.

Triggering events also have a second more important place in your career development. If you've mapped out your career plan, and have successfully filled in the gaps, triggering events can tell you when to execute the next part of the plan. *Once I have done three years of XX, then I will transfer to this other group. Once I have children, I will move to an 80% work week.* And for some individuals, *If XX occurs, I will leave.*

Told by Your Manager That You Don't Have a Future

There are wonderful urban legends about incompetent managers who leave a photocopied lay-off notice on an employee's chair, or who leave a voicemail with the bad news. These stories are not what we are talking about here.

Rather, consider this scenario: although you have had a certain degree of success so far, you don't exactly love your job. At the same time, the hierarchical nature of the business means that there are fewer opportunities for advancement. Your manager asks whether you have considered where your career is taking you, and whether your current path is the one that will let you reach your goals. If your manager is tactful, they may continue the conversation, suggesting that your key strengths in A and B are not what is needed within the organization, and that they are not certain where your next role may be. If your manager isn't tactful, they will tell you that you are at the end of your line, and you have about a year to find something elsewhere.

Whichever type of manager you have, they are sending you two very important messages:

1. It is you who are responsible for your career planning, not them.

2. Start looking for another job: you are no longer on the "A list" of employees, and you will receive fewer (if any) choice assignments during the next year.

TRIGGERING EVENT: This type of conversation is a very powerful, and sometimes scary, triggering event. The solution isn't to quit your job before this conversation happens. The solution is to develop a career plan, and then discuss it with your manager: how can they help you achieve your goals?

An important note: If you have this type of conversation, it is important to understand precisely what is being said. Are you officially been given notice that your employment will come to an end a year from that date? Are you being told that you are, in effect, being demoted? Both of these are important from a legal perspective. If the company is seeking to disengage from you, it may have certain financial obligations to you under employment law.

Keeping Up with the Joneses

Competition and comparison can be very powerful allies. You compare yourself with others in your graduating class, and push harder so that you excel. More so than pressure from a manager, competition can push you to achieve far more than you ever thought possible. You keep up with the Joneses not only on the job, but also with how you spend.

Competition and comparison can be powerful allies. They can also be dangerous.

Unwittingly, you are implicitly measuring yourself against others' goals, not your own. When you began your career, this wasn't a big issue; so long as you were climbing up the ladder, everything was okay. But after a few years, you may have started to recognize that your career goals and others' career goals were not the same. (You also probably realized that buying things doesn't bring enduring happiness.)

Often times, young men and women go into the same business or profession as their parents, whisked there with strong parental expectations or pressure. Again, after a certain time, they may also recognize that their career goals and their parents' goals are not the same.

TRIGGERING EVENT: When you realize that you are in charge of setting your goals, and yet your current path is someone else's. Consider making a change when others' expectations are no longer as important as your own and when it is no longer important to be keeping up with the Joneses.

You Get a Kick in the Head

One day, leaving the office, I stopped to say goodbye to my manager. He was in his mid- to late 50s, brilliant, and full of energy and ideas. That day, he looked ashen. He had just learned of a colleague's sudden heart attack and death. The heart attack victim was his age. While he was certainly sad about losing a friend, this was the first of his generation to pass away, and he recognized that it could easily have been him who had the heart attack. This was a kick in the head. Although he is now well into his 60s and still working, he exercises each day and is far healthier than he was at that time. Guess why.

What other types of *kicks* are there? A personal medical crisis. A family member diagnosed with a terminal disease. The birth of your first child or the death of a parent. Maybe your spouse wants a divorce. Perhaps someone "untouchable" gets fired. Or maybe you get passed over for that promotion.

TRIGGERING EVENT: Whether the news is good or bad, it effectively jolts you out of your complacency and causes you to think differently, perhaps for the first time in years.

The Bluebird Principle

A bluebird is an opportunity. It flies in the window, sings its beautiful song ("Make money and have fun"), and waits for you to do the one thing required for it to take flight. Unfortunately, human nature is what it is; although we recognize the opportunity, we often don't believe it when we see it. Perhaps this is laziness, perhaps it is pride; whatever the reason, we let the opportunity fly away.

The window of opportunity stays open only so long.

When I started giving my children an allowance, I made a deal with them: if they saved half of their allowance, I would double their savings. Care to guess how rarely the payout was made? The Bluebird Principle starts at a very young age!

101

We aren't always afflicted with this laziness; sometimes we grab the Bluebird and we reap the rewards, like my friend who purchased the retail martial arts supply store.

When it comes to our careers, what are some examples of Bluebirds? A manager mentions, "If only we knew how to solve problem XYZ" – and you know exactly how to solve it. You see an advertisement for a not-for-profit board position – and you have the exact experience required for the position. While on vacation overseas you see a tremendous concept – and your clients could profit handsomely if they knew about it for the domestic market.

Each of these examples has one thing in common: if you don't take action, the Bluebird will fly away. The window of opportunity closes at the end of the proverbial day.

So how can you avoid the Bluebird Principle? This is a bit like asking the question about how to avoid procrastination and laziness! Develop your career plan, and then act on your career development priorities. If a Bluebird disrupts those plans, then don't let process get in the way. Grab it.

Career Possibilities: Final Thoughts

How strongly you identify with many of the issues described here depends on your experience. At this point, at least in your mind, you should be making progress on your career plan:

- You have a decent written inventory of your skills and experience (SkillChecks and Reality Check Interviews).
- You understand – through the Personal Balance Sheet – your overall priorities.
- You understand – through the Job Quality Checklist – the attributes of your current position.
- While you may not know exactly what your next role may be, you recognize there are some things that should be done, both personally and professionally.

FOCUS

- There are many, many options that are available. Some will hold more personal interest than others, but all of these options can be possibilities, if you want them to be. On the other hand, don't be swayed by the romantic notion of change: any switch from what you are currently doing means assuming a certain degree of risk.

- Look out for Bluebirds and Triggers.

- Don't bother with the Joneses: define your own goals instead of using others'.

- If you get kicked in the head, use it as a catalyst for action. Particularly if the kick is painful, avoid emotional paralysis by focusing on moving forward.

Looking at the Options

With so many options, how to consider which is the best one? You've already started the process with the Reality Check Interviews; you can now use all the other frameworks to guide your decision.

Once you've determined your career plan, you will have defined your basic direction; it then becomes infinitely clearer how to use your time between now and when your goals are achieved.

Chapter 12:
Choosing Your Goal

CHAPTER IN A FLASH: *Choose your goal by applying the frameworks (Personal Balance Sheet, Job Quality Checklist, Reality Check Interviews, etc.) that you've completed earlier to each of the different options.*

Let's close the argument for good about whether you should work on a career plan. Fact: everyone will leave their current employer; at the limit, it will happen when you retire, many years from now. By retirement, you will want to make sure that all of your Personal Balance Sheet goals have been met. If you leave earlier, then deciding on (and preparing for) your next steps is equally important. In both cases, a career plan – and balance – is needed. If you don't manage your career, by the end of it, you may find that it has managed you precisely into a place you do not want to be.

So, of all the different possibilities, how to decide what's next?

One of my early managers, a financial wizard, gave me some advice: "You can only swim upstream for so long, before packing it in." One of my later managers, a marketing guru, also gave me some advice: "Winners always differentiate themselves, like the fish that swims upstream." There are truths in both of these statements: the common element is that the power of choice rests with you. You can differentiate yourself. You can decide when to pack it in. And you can choose your personal level of success.

What has given you your success to date? Was it your drive, education, experience, acumen, or just plain luck? Whatever it happens to be, your personal strengths (and a bit of luck) will be what continues to drive your success. The challenge, of course, is making the right choice and then converting idea into action.

Seventeen Career Possibilities

- Maintain the course
- New field/practice, industry, or function
- Staff rotations
- Non-traditional work arrangements
- Sabbaticals
- Join a client
- Move to Government, Regulator, Institute, Association, etc.
- Boomerang/Returnee
- Start-up/Entrepreneur
- Consultancy/Free Agent
- Purchase an Existing Business
- Trading Up: Working at another large organization
- Trading Down: Working at a smaller organization
- Earn a grad degree or professional certification (full or part-time)
- Volunteer/Community service work
- Stay at home with kids or parents
- Do something non-traditional

Earlier in the book, you went through a number of diagnostic exercises to help determine capability (SkillChecks, Reality Check Interviews), and exercises that expose context (Personal Balance Sheet, Job Quality Checklist). We will now use the results of these same exercises for a different purpose: helping you consider the next step in your career.

Right from the start, you can probably cross a few of the options off the list. For example, you may already have a graduate degree, or you may have no desire to be a homemaker. Or you might have some good ideas about what your next role should be. If this is the case, still go through the exercise, but choose a slightly different question:

> **Identify career development activities that will move you closer to your goals.**

- What would be the job *after* the next job?
- If I can't have my first choice, what would my second one be – my contingency plan?

Even if you are crystal clear, going through this exercise will help you identify the career development activities that will help you achieve your goals that much faster.

If you are certain that you will be making a change, and you're looking to be open-minded about exploring options, now is the time to be asking "Why not?" for each option. What would it take for you to actually choose a particular option? **For each option, write one paragraph describing the changes in your life that would be needed in order to be successful with that option.**

Another question concerns the criteria, other than "gut," that we should use to make the right choice. Thankfully, you have completed most of the heavy lifting earlier. You will use the SkillChecks, Job Quality Checklist, Personal Balance Sheet, and the Reality Check interview notes to filter the options. (Hint: if you haven't completed these diagnostic exercises in earnest, now would be a very good time to do so!) I certainly wouldn't suggest immediately making a choice based exclusively on these filters; as discussed at the very beginning of the book, their purpose is to act as objective criteria – data points – that can function as a counterpoint to your "gut" instinct. Feel free to make any decision you wish; with more information there is less risk.

Engage the infrastructure of your organization

Beyond your drive and the other factors listed above, a key reason for your success has been your work environment over the last number of years. Think back to "the way you were" five to ten years ago. While you may have been proud of your accomplishments at that time, you now recognize how far you've come. The investment that the organization has made in you has been intense: not just formal training, but the mentoring and coaching, the nature of your tasks assigned, the quality of your colleagues, and so on.

If you are thinking of leaving the organization, some food for thought: the business world is very small, and you will be working (and networking) with your colleagues in the future:

- You may want back in.
- You may need their support for references.
- You may need their technical support.
- You may engage them as advisors.
- You are likely friends with many of them.
- You will be part of a network of former employees (an *alumni network*).

With your future success likely riding on your relationship with a (possible) former employer, it is prudent to engage the proper channels within the firm during the career planning process; you may find a surprising openness. And if there isn't, then no harm done either.

Review SkillChecks

Recall, when you initially did the SkillChecks, it was in the context of where you are at the present time. Let's now use the same information, but in the context of what will come next. For example, from SkillCheck I:

- Have you veered away from the area of your initial training and are interested in "returning to your roots"? Do any of the options suggest that this may be possible?
- Was there something from earlier in your career (or education) that interested you, but you never followed up on, and that is related to a current opportunity?
- Which options take advantage of your "excellent" skills?
- Which options have most in common with the most fun parts of your previous positions?
- Which options incorporate your non-work interests?
- Which options should have a lower priority because you are not strong in those areas?

Each SkillCheck I question can generate many different career possibilities.

As you review, consider this SkillCheck I question more closely: "What non-work activities provide you the most satisfaction? What is it about these activities that interest you?" Your answer can provide valuable clues if you are looking to change career directions. Perhaps you enjoy traveling or working with children. Maybe you like working with your hands or being outdoors.

If you like being on stage, for example, that might indicate several interesting career possibilities: instructing aerobics, teaching school, going into television journalism, or acting. While doing any of these directly might be hard to picture, *indirect* career options relating to this list might be more realistic: opening an aerobics studio, being the CFO of a private school, negotiating acquisitions for a media outlet, or providing financial planning for actors.

Rank each option based on your SkillChecks, Job Quality Checklist, Personal Balance Sheet, and Reality Check Interview notes.

A middle manager coaching client was uncertain of her next step, but she knew that she definitely wanted a change. Her key strengths were her financial acumen and ability to develop strong relationships. Using the SkillCheck I questions, she realized that her personal interests were in the community. This provided the impetus for exploration, which eventually led to a position as director of development for a non-profit organization.

For each of the SkillCheck I questions, pull together a list of potential career possibilities, along with any indirect career options that relate to them. SkillCheck II also suggests some criteria:

- Which options relate directly to areas where you are considered a "guru"?
- Which options might have lower priority because they rely on skills where you only have gaps?

After answering these questions for both SkillChecks, and completing a list of potential career possibilities, review the options again. Have a number been eliminated? Has the priority list changed?

Review Job Quality Checklist

When you first did the Job Quality Checklist, you did it for your existing job. At this point, the Job Quality Checklist can be used to contrast each option.

For example, if the idea of being an entrepreneur and starting your own business appeals to you, how might the actual "job" rate against these criteria? Effectively, each dimension (Fun, Challenge, Like your colleagues, Goals, Balance, and Compensation) is an additional criterion that you can use. The example table shown below is a generic, high-level analysis you should do for each alternative.

***Job Quality Checklist*: Entrepreneur**

FUN: At the macro level, since you're doing something of your own choice, of course it is fun! Peel back the layers, however, and there will likely be some major ups and downs. For example, as the president, it's fun. As the janitor and mailroom clerk, maybe not so much.

CHALLENGE: You'll be doing many tasks for the first time; you'll also be playing new organizational roles for the first time. No problem with challenge here.

LIKE YOUR COLLEAGUES: Since you are choosing them yourself, this is likely not a problem. And if you really, really don't like them, you can always let them go. Ironically, the problem with being an entrepreneur may be that you do not have enough colleagues, at least in the very beginning stages. You will have to find your role models somewhere else: networking meetings, suppliers, and customers.

GOALS: You would need to answer this one in your own context. Presumably, some options move you closer to your goals than others.

BALANCE: Starting a business and looking for balance? In practically all cases, there is *no* balance as an entrepreneur. Of course, you might be different, but expect to give up almost everything in order to grow your business. After the business stabilizes, though, your time is yours to use as you wish.

COMPENSATION: At the beginning, don't look for a big payday. Being an entrepreneur is all about the chase: building something that has enduring value, and then capturing that value when it has matured. If you are the type of person who is worried about certainty of personal income, and who won't be able to sleep at night because of fears of not making payroll, this dimension isn't looking good for you. And of course, there is the risk of failure, personal embarrassment, and financial ruin. On the other hand, the possibility of failure can be tremendously motivating.

When you go through this exercise yourself, it should be more specific and more "me-centric." Think about how different this analysis might be for a retail store compared to an advertising agency or a brokerage house.

Also, the more refined your business idea is, the more relevant your analysis will be.

After you complete this review (Fun, Challenge, Like your colleagues, Goals, Balance, and Compensation) for each of the options, some may fall off the list, while others may look more interesting. Spend some time to rank each based on your relative interest. Short cut: save some time and do this exercise only for those alternatives where there is a real possibility.

Review Your Personal Balance Sheet

How does each option move you toward your next goal, along each Personal Balance Sheet dimension of Community, Family, Intellectual, Spiritual, Physical, Financial, and Career? Some options will move you faster, others more slowly.

The issue isn't how quickly you might realize a goal; the issue is *how your balance will change* from the status quo if you go down any particular path. Questions that follow include whether the balance realignment is acceptable to both you and your family. Is there a time element to any of the options – would the balance shift over time? Using the entrepreneur example from above, the first year or two are "make or break" times, and you will have to pay a price with your balance. Several years later, others may be doing most of the work and your balance will be different yet again.

How will your balance change if you choose a particular option?

Look at the final column of your Personal Balance Sheet, where you wrote down your criteria for success. Consider these criteria yet again: for each option you might choose, which Personal Balance Sheet dimension will be satisfied and which will not?

You may be considering eliminating some options just because you're not willing to pay the price. Rather than discarding options so quickly, consider how you can mitigate the "price" of each potential discard. Perhaps, using the entrepreneur example again, doing it with a partner might help. Or perhaps you should explore financing alternatives: do you look for external funding first, or try to grow the business on a shoestring before approaching lenders?

When you have completed this analysis, revise your rankings of each alternative if you need to do so.

Review Reality Check Interview Notes

It's likely the results of the interviews have already figured prominently in your planning and ranking activities. But now is the time to review your rough interview notes again.

COMMON THREADS: These are the common comments made by many of your interviewees that struck a chord in you. Perhaps they all identified similar strengths. Perhaps they all saw you operating in a particular role, or position, or industry vertical. Are any of these in common with the options you are considering? If yes, great. If no, ask yourself why; if you feel comfortable with the answer anyway, then don't worry about it.

DISSENTING OPINIONS: While most of your interviewees saw you one way, perhaps one or two people saw something that others didn't. Maybe they were in the best (or only) position to notice a particular skill or unique ability. Does this ability point more to one or another of the options?

After considering the common threads and dissenting opinions, re-rank each of the options. Hopefully, at this point, one or two of them are looking more like favorites.

Making Your Choice

Remember that the vast majority of people stay within their organization for years; for some of this group, career planning is focused on preparing for a promotion within their current career path. For others, career planning is focused on developing depth. If you fall into these categories, remember that the prudent career planner also considers development in the context of the job after the next job, and in the context of a contingency.

The majority of people stay within their organization for years.

What if you still have no idea which option best fits? Did you go through each of the diagnostic exercises (SkillChecks, Job Quality Checklist, Personal Balance Sheet, Reality Check Interviews), entirely and honestly? The thinking time that these require is what generates their value. Consider redoing one or more of them, at a greater depth, especially if you just "scanned" the exercises earlier.

If you still find it difficult to commit, even to maintaining the course, don't be stressed about it. Choose an alternative as a proxy goal, and as you fill in the gaps (Chapter 14), you will develop more confidence in your decision, and with this confidence, you'll also develop the courage to commit. If you become less enamoured with this proxy goal, consider yourself fortunate: you've ruled out an alternative, invested in yourself along the way, and still have time to choose a newer, more appealing proxy goal.

What if it is hard to choose between two alternatives? Assuming they are ranked very closely on all the scales above, your analysis has to go one step further. First assess the different risk and return levels between the two front-runners. Then consider how different the preparation and gap-filling for each alternative would be. All other things being equal, if one alternative requires significantly less preparation, then choose it! Once you have added these new variables (risk/return and preparation effort) to the mix, one of the options should move slightly ahead.

What if you have decided on an option (say, to be an entrepreneur), but you don't know what *type* of business to start? Go back to your SkillChecks, and look at where you are rated a guru. Review your Reality Check Interview notes, and look at the common threads. Did your interviewees suggest (or even hint) at something? And finally, consider asking your friends and family for their suggestions, again. You never know what might come up.

Only when the trigger is pulled is your choice actually locked down. Your "choice" up to this point is important only *for the purposes of your planning*. And as you fill in the gaps, plans can, and will, change.

FOCUS

- All the direction-setting exercises you have completed (SkillChecks, Job Quality Checklist, Personal Balance Sheet, and Reality Check Interviews) can now be re-used as personalized criteria for planning your next steps.

- Using them this way, you may find you need to go back and revise some of your earlier work. This is to be expected: as your direction becomes more focused, your analysis demands greater precision as well.

- In the end, it will be your passion that fuels your success. So despite all the exercises and logic, your career plan should head you in the direction of the option that has captured your heart as well as your mind.

Chapter 13:
The Mechanics of Change

CHAPTER IN A FLASH: *If you've decided to make a change, don't expect an exit package from your employer – look at it from their perspective: why should they pay? This chapter also addresses the issue of financial risk and how to mitigate it by using a rainy day fund, some cost-savings measures, and for entrepreneurs, alternative sources of funding.*

Being prepared is one thing, but making a change is altogether something else. Consider re-reading the section on triggering events. As you have refined your direction considerably since triggering events were introduced, you should have some ideas as to what the likely triggers would be for your particular situation.

Write them down! Challenge yourself; if you come up with ten potential triggering events, try to add five others. Of course, *the* trigger may eventually be very different from any of these. The trigger may come at the most unexpected time, but by writing down a list of potential ones, you will at least be sensitized to their possibility.

Exit Packages

When a company is looking to reduce employee headcount, they will often offer generous exit packages (sometimes called "severance") to those they wish to let go. Less frequently, a company may offer a general package open to anyone who fits into a particular category. As an example, older employees, who are often more costly than their younger peers, may be asked to consider early retirement and would be given an exit sweetener to make it appealing.

A number of factors determine headcount requirements within an organization:

- **Economic outlook:** The better the economy, the higher the demand for resources.

- **Account planning:** The more forecast demand, the higher the demand for resources.

- **General recruitment strategy:** Either hire resources, and then sell work to keep them busy, or sell work, and then quickly hire resources to deliver.

- **Other factors,** such as natural attrition, skill and seniority requirements, labor market competitiveness, etc.

Depending on how these factors play out in your organization (or maybe your business unit), your employer may choose to offer you an exit package or not. As well, your employer may decide that they no longer want you as an employee; the cost of firing you is also a severance payment. The legal issues surrounding this are beyond the scope of this book: if you are offered a package, make sure that you get competent advice from a lawyer who specializes in employment law before agreeing to it.

The flip-side of exit packages are retention bonuses. These are often implemented during times of great change, when employee retention is critical to the short-term success of the business.

If you have decided to leave, and you are hoping to *double dip* by getting an exit package at the same time as getting a job elsewhere, consider how an employer would see your request. From their perspective:

> Exit packages are great, but it's easier to get another job when you are still gainfully employed.

- They actually enjoy working with you – so why pay you to go?

- They don't relish the time and cost of finding your replacement – so why invite the extra expense and hassle?

- They see the unique value that you add to the organization – so why pay you to go?

- Your high salary and years of service translate into a large sum – so why volunteer to pay it?

- If you are going to leave anyway – why incur the expense voluntarily?

- They know that your employment contract specifies no payment at all in case of a voluntary departure – so no matter the above, there aren't any contractual obligations to pay.

While there surely are strategies to try to "get" a package (giving less effort, working yourself out of a job, etc.), each is fraught with risk. If you've exhausted internal opportunities, and you've decided that your next job will be elsewhere, then focus on your next job – don't play games with your current employer. It will distract you from your bona fide job search efforts and it may have an adverse effect on your reputation. Put things into perspective: if you choose to leave, in most cases they don't owe you anything at all, and they've got many good reasons for not giving you a thing. Don't be bitter about losing something you never had.

If you are lucky enough to get an exit package, remember that it is not without cost. Especially if you are looking for another corporate position, being recruited away from your current employer is far easier than looking for a job when you don't have one. If you are "packaged out," you are no different than the legions of other unemployed. That being said, if you have a career plan, you will be one giant step ahead.

Standing Up for your Rights

The above discussion assumes that you are successful, have decided to leave, and maybe even have a job offer in hand. You were hoping to double dip by getting an exit package at the same time. But what happens if you are being laid off or demoted?

Many organizations are unaware of their obligations under employment law, or choose to ignore them.

Many organizations are unaware of their obligations under employment law, or choose to ignore them. If the company has decided to let you go, it is in the best interests of all parties to disengage professionally and fairly.

A few years ago, a coaching client was informed that she would be laid off. This happened during her maternity leave, in a jurisdiction that required her position to be held open for her while she was on leave. She was given a "standard" severance package, which was both minimalist and didn't take into account her maternity leave rights. She sought legal counsel to understand more about the requirements under law and ultimately received a fair exit package.

Her organization learned something about employment law and maternity benefits that will ultimately benefit future employees. She learned about employment law, but also a more important lesson: done properly, you gain respect for standing up for your beliefs.

How to Afford It?

A number of career alternatives involve either a reduced income or, in the case of the entrepreneurial options, possibly no income. One of the key questions is about the financial viability of your choice: in other words, how do you afford to do what you want to do? You might be thinking, for example, of the following questions:

- What if I trade up to a bigger company, it doesn't work out, and I'm on the street?

- How can I afford to start a new business; I can't make ends meet as it is!

- What will happen to my house if I can't make the payments? How can I pay for my vacation/health care/kid's education/etc. if things go wrong?
- etc.
- etc.

The financially toughest of all the options are the ones that are designed to reduce your income: these include moving to a reduced work week, and taking a leave to raise children or care for elderly parents. Starting a business is also financially tough, as primary funding often will come from… you. Starting a business also means paying yourself less until the business is self-sustaining. Whether you are choosing a corporate move or an entrepreneurial one, or are reducing your income for other reasons, the following suggestions can reduce your stress immeasurably.

What's the Worst That Can Happen?

Several years ago, hiking high on a mountain pass, I made the big mistake and looked down. When I did that, several small rocks shifted underfoot, fell off the narrow trail, and were pulverized as they fell hundreds and hundreds of feet to the bottom of the valley. Needless to say, I watched the path of the falling rocks and imagined my body following the same route. And that would be the end of my illustrious hiking career.

When it comes to change, we often limit ourselves by perceived risk.

When it comes to career change – or even a promotion – our potential is often constrained by how we imagine risk. The key word here is *imagine*. We think that the worst case would be the end of us – like my hiking adventure.

Is there an easy way to avoid the problem of imagination? Ask "What's the worst that can happen?" Stating the risks explicitly is the first step in mitigating them.

When I left my first long-time employer to start a business, I asked this very question. The answer was that if things didn't work out, we would sell the car, sell the house, and move into my parent's basement. I'm not sure if this was one of the motivators that eventually drove me to success, but naming the worst-case scenario certainly helped demystify it.

Set Up a Rainy Day Fund

The concept is simple: save three to six months of income, just in case. If you lose your job, so the theory goes, your rainy day fund can pay expenses until you find your next job.

Unfortunately, many people don't have the discipline to save. Those who do have discipline realize that it makes more sense to pay down mortgages and other debt than to keep the rainy day funds in a low-interest-bearing savings account. Nevertheless, if you can save a bit each month, or if you can borrow against your equity, a rainy day fund provides both the practical advantage of a safety net and a tremendous psychological boost.

Consider dipping into your rainy day fund during your transition period. For example, if you are moving to another corporate position, maybe the rainy day fund pays for new clothes; maybe it pays for a golf club membership. If you are moving to an entrepreneurial role, the rainy day fund might be used to supplement your salary until the business can stand on its own. If you are moving to a reduced work schedule or a seasonal work schedule, consider using the rainy day fund to help you adjust to your new budget regime.

A rainy day fund provides a critical safety net.

Budgeting

Preparing a detailed personal budget is critical. It may be that you have never needed to budget before, but just as it does in a business setting, a personal budget instills a tremendous sensitivity and discipline. From a more practical standpoint, a budget can let you know the size of your financial cushion and free you from worrying unnecessarily.

If you make a change, your budget will follow a different income and expense pattern. The objective of budgeting is to develop discipline: both in the making of the budget and in the keeping of it. Consider the following factors as you start to prepare:

SEVERANCE AND FINAL PAY: Have you calculated exactly how much severance you may receive, if any? Will your final pay include accrued vacation pay, bonuses, commissions, expense reimbursement, and any claw-backs? Also, don't forget to consider the *after-tax* amount you will actually receive.

INCREASE YOUR NON-EMPLOYMENT INCOME: This can mean anything from changing your investment mix so it provides more income than capital growth, renting out your cottage or rooms in your house, to switching back to a dual-income household, if you currently have only one person in the workforce. If you have adult or teenage children whom you are supporting, insist that they contribute to the family finances too.

REDUCE LIVING COSTS: Where does all your money really go? Consider looking at your last three months' expenditures and categorizing them. What can be deferred until your new position is more certain or your business is on stable ground? What expenses must you really incur at all? Often, we find that our spending has naturally reached the level of available funding. If we reduce the available funding, can our spending be reduced as well?

There are many ways to reduce your budget. Here are a few obvious ones:

- Eat out less often; when you do eat out, go to less expensive restaurants.
- Postpone expensive vacations.
- Avoid lavish gifts and personal trappings.
- Reduce or eliminate the use of non-essential services (e.g., esthetics, cleaners, nannies, gardeners, and others).
- Postpone any non-essential and luxury expenditures for at least three months.

Reduce your cash requirements by questioning every expenditure.

- Start conserving energy around your home.
- Reduce allowances for teenage children, and cut them completely for adult children.
- Do your own laundry instead of sending it to a service.

If the cash crunch is tough, there are certainly more drastic changes you can make:

- Give up or suspend club memberships.
- Trade in your car for a less expensive one.
- Sell your house and move into a less expensive one.

Be Cheap on Administrative Expenses

Each expenditure you make should be for something immediately necessary, especially when the spending is on overhead. Shopping at the Big Warehouse for a case of paper clips makes no sense, if a single box of 100 will do you. Don't laugh – I've seen it. (I've also seen cases of batteries, cases of cello tape, and cases of file folders.)

Do you need the absolute latest laptop? The most expensive BlackBerry? The fanciest home office desk furniture? Most people go to office supply stores for home office furniture; why not check out second-hand office furniture dealers, where higher quality furniture can be found for a fraction of the price?

Every penny saved on overhead buys you time; every penny saved on overhead ends up in your pocket. If you really want one of those whiz-bang laptops, reward yourself with it when the business can truly afford it. Side benefit: you'll appreciate it more then too.

For Entrepreneurs: Seed Capital

Often great ideas are stopped in their tracks because of a roadblock, either real or perceived. The initial capital for an enterprise – seed capital – sometimes fits into this category. Where to find it? Entire books have been written on properly financing your enterprise. The purpose of the list below is to illustrate that there *are* many sources of money, and that these sources are often overlooked.

- General savings.
- Retirement nest egg.
- Second mortgage on house.
- Family and friends.
- Former employer.
- Cash value of life insurance policy.
- Founding clients/Development partners.
- Key suppliers.
- Banks and leasing companies.
- Government grants and loans.
- Early-stage private investors (sometimes called Angel Investors).
- Partners.
- Other financial sources (venture capital companies, merchant banks, etc.).

FOCUS

- Keep your eye out for triggering events.
- Exit packages can help, but think of them only as a bonus, not an entitlement.
- Financial prudence pays off: start with a rainy day fund, develop a budget, and keep administrative expenses as low as possible.

Achieving Your Goals

Several years ago, my wife and I were vacationing in Europe. We spent two weeks driving through many different countries, stopping in one small town or another before moving to the next. We had only one constraint: we needed to end up in Frankfurt for our flight back home.

It was an excellent vacation: we took roads just because they were there. We stayed in small bed-and-breakfasts when our driving days were over. It was liberating to be without a plan. On the flip-side, there was stress: we forgot our maps and travel guides back home, and we couldn't quite find replacements in English. As a result, we really didn't know what the next day – or hour – might bring.

This strategy might be appropriate for vacations in Europe, but it certainly isn't the way to manage your career. Without a map or guide, you can take any road outside your door. With enough trial and error, you might even get to where you want to go. A proper map will reduce the number of wrong roads, reduce the amount of backtracking, and reduce your frustration along the way.

To be successful in your career requires a plan – and not a high-level, theoretical one. What are the specific things that you will do between now and your next milestone? What short-, medium-, and long-term commitments will you make to yourself? How, specifically, should you do networking – and why does it matter? And how do you engage those within your organization – your manager, HR professionals, and others – to help you achieve your goals?

The next several chapters will answer these questions and review the mechanics of achieving your goals.

Chapter 14:
Filling in the Gaps

CHAPTER IN A FLASH: *This chapter lists many of the possible things that you can do to prepare yourself for achievement, along with a description of some obstacles. Often, one of the greatest impediments to our personal success is our own self-image, and the labels we accept.*

Several years ago, I was giving my first major presentation to the senior executives of my parent company. By the time I started speaking, the number of people in the room almost tripled. Naturally I thought it was the critical nature of my presentation that drew people in. It wasn't until afterwards that one of my supporters told me the truth. "It isn't a miracle that everyone magically showed up: I've been priming the pump about this presentation all month."

Something special happened between the time I knew about the presentation and the time I delivered it: I filled in the gaps. I had written the presentation, prepared the slides, and gone through extensive rehearsals. And at the same time, my supporters made sure that I was on the agenda and the room was filled. If all of these hadn't happened, success would be a function of chance, not preparation.

There is a time of special opportunity from when you've set your direction, to when your goals are achieved.

This same concept is central when it comes to developing your career. There is a time of special opportunity that exists between the time you've set your direction and when your goals are achieved: filling in the gaps. If you are thinking about changing jobs, consider this: without filling in the gaps, you will likely not be considered for that next role. And ironically, these gap-filling activities are precisely what will make you more valuable to your current employer! Either way, the ideas in this section of the book are critical: spend time on activities that move you closer to your goal.

Everyone recognizes the maxim of *no risk, no return*. And everyone recognizes there is risk when contemplating a change from the status quo. But that doesn't mean you should take risks that can be mitigated.

While it may seem strange, many of these risk-mitigating and preparatory activities have more to do with *you* than with your career goal. That is why filling in the gaps is also so important for those who are looking to maintain the course and develop a deeper knowledge in their areas of expertise. There are several reasons for this:

- You've spent most of your career in one place, and you've taken on many of the characteristics and habits of that organization. Some of these, such as *procrastination*, *busywork*, and your *self-image*, may need examination.

- Before committing to any change, you may be able to try it out, perhaps on a special project, or perhaps with a non-profit group, without worrying too much about making a big mistake and poisoning the well.

- Whether you're moving to another organization, starting one of your own, or looking for a promotion or transfer, the product people are buying is *you*. Initially you may not have the skills or internal network of support that you are used to; anything you can do to improve yourself beforehand will pay dividends handsomely. Every investment you make improves the product and reduces your risk.

You Can Control Only What You Can Control

As a teenager, I had a summer job in a hardware store. Since I had to take two buses to get there, timing was always a bit of a gamble. This was a problem because the manager got terribly upset (e.g., "You're fired") if staff members weren't punctual. One day, when I was waiting for the first bus, feeling stressed about the time, it struck me. No matter how much I worried, and how many times I paced back and forth, the bus wasn't going to reach the stop any earlier. And when the bus did come, I certainly wouldn't be able to make it drive any faster. So I got out my book and was able to read a few chapters en route. When I had that epiphany, I also realized that the worry (and stress) of being late wasn't caused by a threatening manager, but rather by me internally.

As you're filling in the gaps, don't worry about what isn't really necessary – and don't worry about what you can't control. Think instead about what is within your power to change. While I couldn't control the speed of the bus once I was on it, I sure could have caught an earlier one.

What is "really necessary" and what is not? Tasks, priorities, people, and processes that help you focus are necessary; anything that distracts you from your goal likely is not.

Think of how your company (or department) has maintained its focus over the years. Conventional wisdom and the business press have spawned dozens of useful sayings: define core competencies, stick to your knitting, customer care, etc. Has your organization adopted any of these? Likely, quite a few. Think of your corporate funding decisions, for example. When there is plenty of cash, new projects tend to be funded; when cash is tight, the oxygen of cash goes only to the most important, core parts of the organization.

As you fill in the gaps, you must start with the most important "core" activities on your list. Then, with diminishing marginal benefit, the less important activities can come later. If an opportunity presents itself – a triggering event – you have to be ready, hopefully with as many of the important gaps filled as possible.

While this is easily said, three obstacles can prevent this from happening: *procrastination*, *busywork*, and *the problem with getting a "B."*

Procrastination

It is ironic that we spend more time on business-related planning than on our personal planning. Why is that? Is it because we've been shown how to do *business*, but no one has shown us how to do *personal*? Or is it because we are procrastinating? Probably a bit of both. This book applies process to career planning, so it can help you organize the *personal*.

Procrastination can be addressed only by first recognizing it, then developing the discipline to avoid it.

Delaying a task needlessly delays your goals.

Every minute that we delay is a minute away from the important things that we must make time for: think of your Personal Balance Sheet. These goals are things we *need* to do, not optional activities that we may *want* to do. When we procrastinate, we substitute required *needs* for desired *wants*: we kill progress!

We sometimes pretend that a task doesn't exist merely because we don't want to see it, like an ostrich with its head firmly in the sand. Once we pluck our head out and look around, what was once a small problem often has grown considerably. When we put off something that is a higher priority, we needlessly add stress to our lives.

Every minute that we delay also adds risk. If a triggering event happens, and we haven't filled enough of the important gaps, success may prove elusive.

Busywork

Have you ever quickly grabbed a chocolate bar and a soft drink for lunch? Busywork is to your time like empty calories are to nutrition. The chocolate bar and soft drink may be tremendously satisfying while you're eating them, but they displace important vitamins and other nutrients that your body needs. Busywork takes up your available time, displacing important priorities that really should be seen to first. In a sense, busywork is a form of procrastination.

Think of the scenario where you have ten things on your task list. One is a critical presentation to a potential client, due two days from now. The other nine items are things that are relatively unimportant, due next week. With effort, you can deal with all nine of them within a few hours. Do you focus exclusively on the presentation, or do you get rid of the nine unimportant items first? Intellectually, most people will say that the presentation is the priority. When it comes to practice, though, there are no shortages of rationales for doing the exact opposite:

- **"Killing the nine little things means I can concentrate on the priority."** This is the *reduce my stress* argument. Think about it: if there is time to do both before the presentation is due, why not do the presentation first – just in case?

- **"If I deal with the nine little things first, then I won't hold up the nine folks who need my input."** This is the *I'm indispensable* argument. Surely having them wait two days isn't going to make a difference? And if one of these nine items becomes critical along the way, you can change your decision as to which item gets your immediate attention at that time.

- **"I've always hated doing presentations; I'll be more comfortable if I do the other stuff first."** This is the *fear and uncertainty* argument. If we are afraid of doing something, because of either a bad experience or inexperience, we think that doing it last will magically increase our confidence level. Logic suggests the opposite: the less comfort we have with a task, the more time we need to do it, and thus the earlier we should start it.

People who do the busywork first tend to use large amounts of personal time to fit in their priorities. Some, having finished their work late at night, have a great feeling of satisfaction for having so much "output." Others are just plain tired.

So how do you avoid the evils of procrastination and busywork? Each person is different. Nevertheless, here are some basic ideas you might try:

- Recognize when you are procrastinating or doing busywork. (Then stop doing it!)
- Schedule (and budget) your time, then keep to that schedule.
- Set up your to-do list the night before.

- Take a course on time management.
- For more suggestions, go to www.PersonalBalanceSheet.com.

You can control only what you can control. If there is a magic bullet against procrastination and busywork, as one of my former managers repeated over and over, it is **Focus – Focus – Focus.**

The Problem with Getting a "B"

If you ask your children, or worse, your children's teachers, whether 70% is an acceptable mark, the answer will likely be "Absolutely: a 'B' is great," followed by the comment that while an "A" would be better, not everyone can get an "A." This attitude, which is where mediocrity gets its start, poisons us both in school and at work. When we evaluate our staff, how many of them are happy with a rating of "meets expectations" and no longer strive for a "superstar" rating? From a management perspective, if we are satisfied with a 70%, is there not a conflict with a "100% customer satisfaction" philosophy?

Would you be satisfied with a pilot who crashes their plane 30% of the time?

No one wants a kick in the pants, but an evaluation of (say) 55% often will spur real change. An effort of greater than 90% usually means a high resolve already exists. A score of 70%, unfortunately, will neither spur change nor is it an indicator of an excellent resolve: hence the problem with getting a "B." If you are right 70% of the time, by definition you are wrong three times out of ten. Would you be satisfied with a surgeon or a pilot doing their jobs wrong 30% of the time? Do you think your clients would be satisfied with that percentage either?

The relevance to us as managers and leaders (and especially in the context of developing your career) is that merely recognizing that 70% is not acceptable will often mark you as different. And the difference between a 70% organization and a 100% organization is the difference between success and failure in what you do next in your career.

While you are doing your day job *and* filling in the gaps, there is no room for anything less than 100% personal effort and excellence. Otherwise, you will be either compromising your current position or reducing your chance of promotion and success.

Opening Closed Doors

One of the ugly things we do, often without realizing it, is label things. Why? It helps us to categorize an item, and later to remember it.

Unfortunately, a funny thing often happens – the item begins to take on the characteristics of the label itself. This is relevant in our context for two reasons: we often label other people, and we unwittingly label ourselves.

Think about the last time you tried a new sport. Did you think, "I am uncoordinated, so this will be tough," or did you think, "I am a natural athlete, so I expect to be good at this?" In either case, your self-label (*uncoordinated* or *athletic*) will have an impact on your mindset, and this mindset will have a real-life impact on your success in that sport. Giving unhelpful labels is something we also do to those closest to us, and unfortunately, our friends and family often will live up to the label: "not good at reading," "can't control their weight," "bad car driver," "doesn't dress appropriately," etc.

It is always satisfying to see someone spring open an artificially closed door. My father, a retired senior executive, had always "recognized" that he was physically not flexible. When it came to sports, he avoided activities that required flexibility and took up ones that emphasized other athletic attributes, such as focus, endurance, and speed. Only after trying Pilates did he realize that he could have developed significant flexibility, if only he had started stretching long ago.

Often, we limit our potential by setting artificially low expectations.

We often live our business lives within the boundaries of the labels we give ourselves. Are we "no good at presentations," "not the best at relationships," or "technically inept"? It is worthwhile examining carefully, and perhaps modifying, our own self-labels, as they may be limiting our ultimate success.

Exercise in Self-Labeling

1. Using a chart similar to the one below, write down all the labels that you think apply to yourself, separating the positive and negative ones.

2. For each of them, write down the first event (or events) that convinced you the label was accurate.

3. Then write down a different event that refuted the negative label.

4. For those negative labels where there is no refuted event, put together a plan to succeed: a plan, which once completed, will prove to you that the negative label no longer holds true. Executing this plan is what opens a closed door.

Negative Labels

Label	First event	Refuted event (or plan)
Unathletic	Always last one picked for team as a kid; dropped Phys Ed as soon as possible	Earned Black Belt as an adult
Insensitive to staff	As first-time manager, staff wanted to transfer	Earned loyalty of subordinates in next management job
Can't do presentations	Messed up presentation when at university, and have avoided presentations since	PLAN: take a public speaking course, videotape presentation rehearsals, present to smaller audiences more frequently to develop comfort

Positive Labels

Label	First event
Great at sales	Sold lottery tickets at high school
Group organizer	Put together band during university
Driven	Client feedback about me as manager on first large assignment

Labeling hurts those outside of work as well. If you have children, have you labeled them too? "Jennifer is a real beauty, while Sam is the thinker in the family."

What if Jennifer develops into a slightly heavier teenager, but brilliant academically? She might become so preoccupied with her appearance that she neglects her true gift of scholarship. Or Sam, who might really like sports but never tries out for the football team because he has to study so hard to maintain his imposed image of being "the thinker."

Look at how you answered your own self-labeling exercise (you did do it, didn't you?). Consider how your career has progressed over the years as you have abided by these labels. Had you missed early promotions because you "weren't the best at relationships"? What if you could rely on the strength of your presentations – instead of avoiding them because you were "always bad at presentations"?

Very early in my career, I took on the role of technology coordinator for my group. Almost 20 years later, after starting my own firm, selling it, and eventually becoming a senior vice-president of a public company, there is still one person from my past who asks (seriously), "How's computers?" whenever he sees me. Clearly, in this person's mind, I have a label. It doesn't limit me because this person is someone I rarely see and whose network is completely different than my own. But what if he were my current manager or a senior executive in my organization? Before panning this person too much, consider whether you have inadvertently given labels to your staff, peers, and managers. Releasing them from their labels will let them stretch their wings – often to your benefit.

Labels often will stay with you for decades, so make sure they are good ones.

As you consider the career options described earlier, remember that the label you give yourself is your label that you give yourself! Leaving negative labels behind is just as important as remembering the positive ones you take with you. **Action: Fill in the gaps by following your plan to remove negative labels. Open those doors!**

Your Personal Balance Sheet – in Action

Earlier in the book, you defined a number of goals along each of the Personal Balance Sheet dimensions: Community, Family, Intellectual, Spiritual, Physical, Financial, and Career. For each of these, you had also defined the criteria for success. While you are filling in the gaps, much of your attention should be focused on the Career dimension. But what about the others?

Most people, when they complete the Personal Balance Sheet, see an embarrassing gap between their goals and accomplishments. Filling in the gaps is not only about developing your career; it is about making sure that your career develops within a chosen-by-you context of balance.

Add a final extra column onto the chart: action plan. For each dimension on the Personal Balance Sheet, review your goals and write down the steps to achieving them. For example, if your Community goal

The sooner you start, the sooner you will reach your goals.

was for greater involvement and you wanted to achieve this by organizing an annual neighborhood fun day, your action plan would define each of the steps necessary to make the fun day happen.

Investing time in other goal-oriented personally-oriented activities is energizing. Once you have reasonable plans against each Personal Balance Sheet dimension, devote time to actually making them happen. Writing a plan doesn't achieve results – executing it does.

Leverage Strengths

Industry

What can you do to increase your profile in your industry? There are a number of opportunities, including the following:

- Being a delegate on a standard-setting body.
- Providing input to regulatory authorities.
- Volunteering in your industry association.
- Teaching a course on your industry at a college or vocational school.
- Writing articles for your trade magazine.
- Public speaking in your field.
- Writing a blog in your area of expertise.

Personal Characteristics

What is it that really has accounted for your success so far? All the diagnostics that you did earlier (SkillChecks, Reality Check Interviews, etc.) should point you in the right direction. What can you do to further reinforce these strengths? Perhaps there is a way to become publicly recognized for them. Look at the industry list (above) for a few ideas. Even if it is just the smallest thing, start something that moves you toward your goals.

Deal with Weaknesses

Strengthen Your Weaknesses

After a certain point in our career, we recognize that more progress can be made by focusing on our strengths and ignoring our weaknesses. While this is true when you're surrounded by elaborate support structures, it isn't exactly true if you've decided to go through a career transition. In fact, the difference between success and failure may depend precisely on how you perform in those areas that are your blind spots.

In high school, what was the one subject you didn't like and avoided as much as possible? Ask yourself today if you feel the same way about the subject, and indeed how much you are currently using those skills. For myself, I dropped physical education as soon as I could, partly because of the demotivating teachers I had, but mostly because I was uncoordinated and not "jock" material. Today, I go to the gym at least 12 hours each week, am very fit, and have earned a Black Belt in karate. For you, perhaps you have begun to be more interested in history, religion, genealogy, or as I have, in fitness. The point: with maturity and experience comes new perspective; a weakness of ten years ago may have caused you to artificially close the door on your development in this area. The "old" weakness lives only in your mind, and not in reality!

Notwithstanding this logic, let us not have the weakness of arrogance: we all have our strengths, and we all have our weaknesses. These weaknesses can be categorized three ways: Skills, Industry, and Personal Style weaknesses.

SKILLS WEAKNESS: Strange as it may sound, I don't enjoy the bookkeeping function. So why bother investing in making me better at something I will always avoid? No doubt, we have all felt this way about certain parts of our jobs at one point, but if you are looking for career growth, you must look at your *skills weaknesses* through a wider lens. Perhaps, in your next role, you will need those skills. Learning to "speak the language" of your weakness may be critical to communicating with functional experts in this area.

Here are some ideas on how to improve your skills knowledge:

- **Take an introductory course.** A number of courses are offered by universities, colleges, private training academies, professional trade groups, etc., that are relatively low cost and relatively high quality. Taking a course provides the extra benefit of giving you a built-in network of those within the field already.

- **Hire a tutor.** For a fairly low cost, you can hire a person to buff up specific areas of weakness. I recently traveled to China for the first time and hired a tutor to help with language skills before I left. While I wish I had hired her earlier, every minute spent learning paid off. The extra benefit of hiring a tutor is that you can call on them for help later, if you find yourself stuck. Unfortunately for me, distance and time zones meant my tutor wasn't available while I was in China.

- **Sign up for a degree program or a professional designation.** Whether or not you decide to complete an MBA, CFA, CISA, or some other acronym, the course work required is usually intense, relevant, and valuable. Be realistic, however, about how much time you can devote to actually completing the course of studies. The objective here is to improve a weakness, not earn the degree. But again, if you are taking a number of courses, you may as well earn the degree or certificate anyway!

- **Arrange for your next assignment at your current workplace to include elements of the skills you wish to develop.** For example, if you have identified project management skills as a weakness, choosing an assignment where these skills must be developed properly, and delivered by you personally, will absolutely ensure that you develop the skills! This same strategy can be used if you volunteer at a non-profit.

- Again, in the context of your current position, put yourself in a position to **manage those with the specific skills that you are weak in.** Get yourself trained as the back-up for your staff.

INDUSTRY WEAKNESS: Perhaps your next move is to an industry where your knowledge, however strong, is from the perspective of an outsider. Or you are contemplating a move to a different industry group within your current organization. While the specifics of how to close this gap would be unique to your situation, here are a few ideas that can help:

- **Trade journals:** Read the last five years' issues, then subscribe to all the trade journals yourself. Old issues are usually available free of charge in the larger city (and college) reference libraries, and sometimes on-line. If your employer has a library, check there as well. The paper version, with all the advertising included, is likely to be more helpful than an on-line version.

- **Industry research:** Arrange to get industry research from investment banks and brokers for your target industry. Usually they write shorter analyses for retail investors, and a more comprehensive analysis for institutional investors. This latter type of research is often difficult to come by, but when available, is excellent. Some trade associations also offer research at no cost.

- **Newsletters:** There are a number of web-based and email-based newsletters and discussion groups; some of these have dozens (or hundreds) of submissions daily, and most of them are available at low or no cost. If there is a digest option, be sure to choose it, otherwise your email box may be inundated with individual messages. Make the newsletters or discussion groups part of your daily reading regime.

- **Commissioned research:** Pay an MBA or PhD student to do a "survey" on the industry you are considering, addressing the industry structure, issues, trends, and key success factors. (You can also consider journalism students.)

- **Gurus:** After becoming reasonably familiar with the industry, purchase two to three hours of time from an industry guru, to validate your understanding of the issues facing the industry. Gurus can come from many places: the publisher of a trade magazine, the financial analyst who has covered the sector for 20 years, the entrepreneur who has "struck it big" more than once, a college professor whose research concentration is in the area, etc. Of course, there will likely be a number of gurus within your organization as well – don't forget them.

- **Jobs:** Take a part-time job in the industry. One of my coaching clients decided that when they retired early, they wanted to open a bed-and-breakfast. They were long on excitement, but short on experience. My counsel was to find a weekend job for a few months working part-time in one. Live the dream, and learn the industry. You may get a bit of a wake-up call.

> Focus on your weaknesses only enough to prevent them from holding your back.

- **Internet Research:** Spend time looking on the internet for the information hubs frequented by those in the industry. Sometimes information can be found in a specific portal, blog, newsgroup, newsletter, or group of sites. Look at resources such as Wikipedia, as well as specialized search engines.

- *Reality Check* **interviewees:** Spend more time with one of the people you interviewed for your Reality Check. Particularly if they have experience in your area of weakness, time with them can be invaluable.

PERSONAL STYLE WEAKNESSES: Arrogant, overeager, too quiet, a pushover, crude, sexist, racist, binary, impatient, too forgiving, too aggressive, meek, headstrong, patronizing, insincere. This list of ugly descriptors can go on for pages. Understanding your *personal style* weaknesses is sometimes a bit touchy, as we each tend to think of ourselves as having "great" – or at least not deficient – personal style. The truth, however, is that it is hard to see ourselves properly in the mirror. Small things that we say can create great dysfunction, and we remain unaware and oblivious. Other behaviors we obsess about, yet they are not important at all. Sometimes, we feel that we don't have a "problem," but perceptions effectively become reality, and therefore still must be identified and addressed.

A good third-party diagnostic is critical. Thankfully, there are at least two that should be easily available: your prior personnel reviews, and the findings from the Reality Check Interviews, completed earlier.

- **Personnel Reviews:** The first step is to get copies of your last five written reviews – something often easier said than done. Re-read these reviews, but instead of remembering the good times (or "that awful manager"), pay close attention to comments that speak to any style weaknesses. Sometimes code words are used, obscuring the real meaning. For example, if you are described as being *a strong advocate of his own views,* perhaps it really means that you tend not to listen well and have a big mouth. Write down all hints of style weaknesses; identification and acknowledgment are the first step to dealing with them.

- **Reality Check Interviews:** While most of these interviews focus on the interviewee, some of the common themes will likely relate to your strengths and weaknesses.

Changing personal style is just about the toughest task you can do. It may also be close to impossible. Nevertheless, sometimes an investment here pays dividends well beyond your job. (Think about your family relationships.) A rational question would be "What is reasonable to achieve?" It is unlikely that a "softie" can be quickly changed into "hard-nosed" overnight, or vice versa. Indeed, your particular skills, *including your weaknesses,* have played an important role in your success to date.

One technique that many find useful is to hire a coach. Properly experienced coaches can highlight areas of your personal style that are weak, and help get you on the road to recovery. They can also help prioritize your career planning activities, and hold you to your commitments.

STYLE FLEXIBILITY: A more practical, and reasonable, approach is to look at your personal style, and then commit to developing a greater *flexibility* of style. If you were able to change your approach to suit the style of the person or groups that you interact with, that would be a major leap forward. Consider: when a team is behind schedule, is it better to browbeat them with pressure, or "buck them up" with encouragement? Each of us as managers has a more comfortable zone of style; in order to develop flexibility, the task is to consider what other types of responses will achieve the same desired goal. Said another way, consider responses other than what usually first comes out of your mouth. At the end of the day, you may do exactly what you had first thought of, but sometimes, you will react differently – and that is the beginning of style flexibility.

We probably should look at something about another personal style weakness: bad habits. If you have them, you must stop them. The list of annoying habits can be endless – for example, everyone has one colleague who doesn't stop picking their nose or teeth, fiddles with their watch, always answers their cell phones during meetings, or is constantly jingling the coins in their pockets. For many, smoking falls into this bad habit category as well. In your current position, those around you (and especially if you have subordinates) usually will tolerate these habits, but if you make a change, you may find that others are far less forgiving.

Your personal style wasn't built in a day, and it won't be changed in one either.

Whether it is a weakness in personal style, or "just" an annoying habit, here are several ideas that may help:

- Acknowledge your weaknesses and bad habits to yourself by writing them down.

- Rank the top three attitudes or behaviors you wish to change. Before you begin each work day, remind yourself of them.

- Prior to reacting with your "gut," put yourself in the other person's shoes, and ask yourself what you could say that would yield the desired result.

- Get a family member, co-worker, or trusted subordinate to give you a private signal whenever the habit shows up.

- Leverage any workplace-provided Employee Assistance Programs for counseling and suggestions.

- Like Rome, your style wasn't built in a day. Recognize that it will take more than a day to change it. In fact, research suggests that you have to repeat the "new habit" 21 times in order for it to stick.

Leaving Your Weaknesses as is

Perhaps you've improved your weaknesses as much as possible, or perhaps time hasn't permitted as much work on your weaknesses as you'd like. There still remains a question: will the sum total of your weaknesses increase your future risks beyond what is acceptable? If the answer is no, then no problem. Remain aware of your weaknesses, but spend your time on other activities. If the weaknesses are relevant to your next position, the only way to address them is to hire (or partner with) someone whose strengths are exactly your weaknesses.

Avoid Planning Paralysis

When we have a great idea, what do we often do? We spend enormous time considering all of the possibilities for failure; we delve deeply into stakeholder analyses, Porter's Five Forces, and just about every other analytical framework around. We spend time doing everything that we can think of, except translate the plan into action. The question is why. Consider these possibilities:

- **Habit:** We've always done it that way.

- **Fear of risk or fear of failure:** Sometimes we think it makes sense to plan out all the possibilities, just so we will know what to do in every conceivable scenario.

- **Fear of the unknown:** Sometimes planning takes the place of action because we're uncertain of what the future may hold. We procrastinate, instead of jumping in the water and learning to swim.

- **Comfort in busywork:** With so much to do before actually executing the plan...

Interestingly, in the software development world, there are two different philosophies for delivering a project. In *RAD* – Rapid Application Development – a working prototype is built and tested, then users provide feedback, which gets incorporated into a second prototype. Users provide more feedback, which gets incorporated into a third prototype, and so on. The development project is completed when the feedback suggests that it is ready for production. An interesting side benefit is that user involvement promotes user ownership and adoption of the end product.

In the other approach, called *Waterfall*, a Requirements Document is produced and signed off by the user community. Then a Functional Specification is produced and signed off. Then a Technical Specification is produced and signed off. Then development starts. Once complete, it is tested, bugs fixed, then "accepted" by the users for production.

While the technology folks will tell you that there are plenty of problems with RAD, it does have two appealing benefits: many opportunities for mid-course corrections, and something visible right from the start. The problem with the Waterfall approach is that when the development phase is complete and the project deployed, the business requirements may have changed dramatically from when the plan was originally agreed to.

When *you* spend so much time planning, rather than acting, your requirements may have changed too. And even if they haven't, with all your attention on planning for the perfect scenario, you may miss an obvious triggering event for an even better scenario.

Another perspective on planning vs. action is the law of diminishing marginal returns, or the *Pareto principle*. It is often simplified to the neat equation of 20% of the effort for 80% of the result. This makes sense, in that most people are not interested in the other side of the equation, which is spending 80% of the effort for a mere 20% of the result.

Spend 20% of your time getting 80% of the benefit, then re-evaluate.

How does this jibe with concepts such as continuous improvement? Once the 80% result is complete, that is precisely the time to look around, check your compass, and possibly do a mid-course correction. At this point, the process can start again, with 20% effort giving us another 80% result. Assuming no mid-course correction, you will now be at a 96% result. And the cycle can continue, until you are at the point where it really doesn't matter about the marginal improvement. RAD once again.

In the context of filling in the gaps, what if an opportunity presents itself earlier than you expect it to? Having spent only 20% of the time doing 80% of the preparation reduces your risk considerably. And having opportunities to do a mid-course correction after spending only 20% of your effort isn't so bad either. While planning is important, action yields results.

FOCUS

- Filling in the gaps refers to the activities that connect now with the time when your goals are achieved.

- Taking charge of your career development means using your time productively from now until you reach your goal – don't let planning paralysis, busywork, or procrastination get in the way.

ACTION CHECKLIST

☐ Your Personal Balance Sheet in Action: add an extra column for your Action Plan.

☐ Complete the exercise in Self-Labeling.

Chapter 15:
The Career Commitment Chart

CHAPTER IN A FLASH: *The Career Commitment Chart is a one-page summary of your goals and your plans to achieve them.*

Several years ago while I was delivering a career management seminar, a participant put up her hand with a complaint: she had been doing career planning for years and nothing had happened. I asked her about her approach, and she explained that she had attended a number of seminars, read a number of books, but nothing had changed. It seemed obvious to me that this person hadn't actually done anything! I politely told her so. No action means no change.

Just as the Personal Balance Sheet contains action items for achieving an appropriate work-life balance, the Career Commitment Chart identifies the positive action items required to achieve your career goals. Of course, the first priority would be to actually define your goals. The SkillChecks and Reality Check Interviews should help you do that. The action items should be specific, tangible activities that will move you closer to your goals.

Short-term goals are those that will help you be successful in your current role. They may be skills that require some polish, or new competencies that you are hoping to learn. Medium-term goals are the ones that will give you breadth and a platform for growth into your next role.

	Career Goal	Action Items	Status/Milestone
Short term (within the year)			
Medium term (next few years)			
Longer term (5+ Years)			

Career Commitment Chart

If you are not sure about the longer term, fill in a proxy goal and work toward that. So much can change in five years anyway; movement toward *something* that you think is your goal will at least get you closer – and provide important knowledge for possible mid-course corrections.

After you have filled in the chart, the next step is to solicit feedback and support from your manager and others. The tighter you can align and integrate your goals with your organization's annual evaluation and objective-setting processes, the easier it will be for you to achieve them. Notwithstanding this, your career plans are a personal responsibility; having little employer support for your career goals does not change your need to have them, nor should it stop you from achieving them. Whether you have support from your manager or not, your mentor and your family should also be used for feedback.

Finally, the Career Commitment Chart needs to be translated into action. This means calendarizing the action items themselves, and following through. Remember that to achieve a medium- or longer-term goal, an Action Item may need to be started early.

If one of your goals was to leave your employer, but you feel uncomfortable showing the chart to them because of this, put in a goal that assumes that you are staying. This will allow you to collect feedback on activities that would be useful if you did stay. And since no one can predict the future (including you), who knows – you may end up staying after all.

FOCUS

- The Career Commitment Chart speaks to your goals, and also your commitments. It is the central career planning document that guides all of your career development activities.

ACTION CHECKLIST

❑ Complete your Career Commitment Chart, and review it with your manager, mentor, and family.

❑ Review/revise your Career Commitment Chart on an annual basis.

Chapter 16:
Talking to Your Manager

CHAPTER IN A FLASH: *This chapter provides example narratives for discussing career planning with your manager. The underlying message behind each conversation is a sensitivity to your manager's requirements: if you can understand how they might see your request, you'll be more likely to be successful with it.*

You can't do it all by yourself. Within every organization there is a support structure that includes your immediate manager, often a more senior manager, often at least one HR professional, and sometimes a mentor or two. This ecosystem can either be engaged by you or ignored at your peril.

Speaking to your manager (or other appropriate person) is required to develop support. They are the ones who can choose your priorities. They are the ones whom others will ask about your performance. And they are the ones who will put you up for promotion – or not.

Typically, these discussions take place within the context of your annual employee evaluation process. For organizations that don't do career planning explicitly within their evaluation process, the discussions sometimes happen informally – or not at all.

Role-play the conversation until you are comfortable.

Unfortunately for you, even when there is discussion on the topic, there often isn't adequate time (or resources) to help you properly evaluate your career goals, and therefore these conversations tend to be brief and focused on the shorter term. The purpose of this book is to help you flesh out your career plan, so that these discussions are productive for everybody.

I Would Like Your Feedback on my Career Commitment Chart

You may be an expert in the field of, say, auditing; in fact, you may have spent your entire career doing this. And the very same thing likely applies to your manager. Neither of you have spent your entire career, every day, working on career planning and Career Commitment Charts. Nor have you each spent your entire career having conversations about careers.

For this reason, your manager may be just as uncomfortable as you discussing the subject. To make the conversation easier, you will probably need to do much of the work. This makes sense, as you are hoping to gain most of the benefit.

Your manager may be just as uncomfortable as you discussing your career.

If the timing works, doing so concurrently with your annual evaluation is certainly convenient. But whether you do it at that time or sometime else, you will need to provide some notice regarding the topic of conversation.

"I have spent some time thinking about my career: what are my next steps? Where do I need to invest the time? What are the possibilities?

"I would like to set up a time to get your feedback on some of my thoughts. Can we schedule a meeting sometime in the next week or so?"

Recognize that when you meet for the first time, you will be talking about your direction; this might be different than subsequent meetings, where you receive feedback on your progress.

"Thank you for meeting with me. I have spent considerable time thinking about what my next steps might be, and I realized that I had to first spend time considering what my career goal itself ought to be.

"I also realized just how much work I will need to do to achieve even my short-term goals. I asked for this meeting because I realize that I can't achieve what I hope to without your feedback. I also realize that I need your support, because some of the things I am interested in doing I have never done before.

"I have put together this action plan – a Career Commitment Chart – that I would like to walk through with you.

"I am pretty certain of my goals, but I don't know if the action steps are really the ones that make the most sense. I would like help from you to validate them, and perhaps to help brainstorm on other ideas that can be incorporated into the plan.

"…in particular, I see the need to develop experience in the area of XYZ, and I was hoping that you would consider adding me to that project…

"Thank you for your time. Would it be okay if I came to you in six months or so, to review progress, and garner any additional feedback…?"

I Would Like to Be Considered for Promotion

There is sometimes a conflict between when you think you are ready for promotion, and when your manager thinks so. But this conflict doesn't need to exist, if you plan it properly. First of all, pretty much everyone is interested in getting a promotion. But not everyone is interested in doing the work to earn it. Therefore, to be successful at getting promoted, spend your time earning it. Have another look at Chapter 11, Career Possibilities, and review the section on Maintaining the Course for specific ideas how. And make sure that you have a realistic Career Commitment Chart.

Well before you consider yourself ready, you will need to do the "ask":

"I am considering my next career steps, and I would like to understand if there are criteria used for promotion to the next level...." Or, *"I am very interested in a promotion to the position of XX, but understand that I have a lot of work to do before I'm ready. Are there specific criteria? What would they be...?*

"Beyond the formal criteria, I'm interested in what it takes to succeed in that new role. That way, I can work backwards, and focus on learning those skills...."

Signal your interest in a promotion at the same time as you signal your willingness to work hard for it.

By asking, you will have done two key things: signalled that you have an interest, and identified the areas where you will need to fill any gaps. Even more importantly, asking in this way can help engage your manager in the process.

Probably one of the most demotivating experiences occurs when you are told that you didn't get a promotion. You may feel some rejection, and you think to yourself: if the organization doesn't want me, then I don't want them! This creates an attitude problem, which hampers your ability to learn from the experience and, if you decide to start an external job search, will hamper your ability to get hired outside too.

What happened during the selection process was simple: they looked at the requirements of the more senior job, and then they looked at you. They determined that you had a greater "gap" than your competition, so therefore the other person was promoted. Insight: by filling in this gap, you can improve your chance of winning the promotion in the future. Right now, your most important task would be to identify that gap: through introspection and discussions with the hiring manager, HR, and others. It is a difficult conversation because of the emotion of the situation, so leave some time (at least a week!) before you start. Here is how that conversation might go:

"I've thought very much about the promotion I've missed, and I now recognize that to be successful in the role in the future, I have a lot of work to do. I wanted to ask for your help identifying some of the areas that I

should concentrate on....

"Thanks. If I were to compare myself to the successful candidate: were there any areas of weakness when you reviewed my experience?

"Is there anything within my current role that you think I should focus more on, in order to develop relevant skills...?

"Can I check back with you, perhaps in four to six months, to touch base on my progress...?"

I Would Like to Move to Another Division

For some managers, when they hear these words, it is no different than "I'm quitting": their minds go into overdrive about how to fill your position. Yet they may also be pleased that you are staying within the organization, as you will be another strong node in their network who can be easily called, whenever necessary.

For managers (and sometimes mentors) who have spent their entire careers in one area, your decision to follow a different path might be felt like a slap in the face. After all, if they could have an excellent career in the area, then surely you can too. Your decision to transfer to another division may be seen as repudiating all of their success – and all of the other advice they have given you over the years.

Once again, the most effective way to talk to your manager about this is well beforehand – so there is no bomb that is dropped. Engage your manager or mentor (and possibly the HR group) in the decision-making process; their experience will give you perspective, and you will need their support (and reference) to change anyway. Consider this approach:

"The exposure (and the client responsibilities) that you have given me over the last several years has been fantastic. One area that I have particularly enjoyed is ABC.

"Recently, I met with a colleague who has been working in that area for some time, and they mentioned that there were some opportunities there that I may be interested in exploring.

"Before I do this, I wanted your perspective: what are the real differences between that division and this one? Had you considered making this type of change earlier in your career? Is there someone that you can recommend I connect with to get more perspective?

"If this area is in my career path, I wanted your feedback on when it would be best to make the change...."

I Would Like to Have a Non-traditional Work Arrangement

Thankfully, most organizations recognize that not everyone fits the 100% standard career model for 100% of their careers. Given the importance of employee retention (and the costs of recruiting and training new staff), many organizations also have formalized guidelines to allow for different approaches.

Be open to your manager's ideas as you present them with yours.

Nevertheless, not all managers are "enlightened," and even if they are, their first concern is covering your responsibilities – not your personal circumstances.

Before you approach your manager, you have to do your homework:

1. Define your preferred non-traditional work arrangement.

2. Define a second choice that is not optimal, but which you would be willing to try.

3. Determine the official policies on non-traditional work arrangements.

4. Look for successful examples of your desired arrangement at your workplace. (And find out from those having the arrangement what the key success factors were.)

5. Identify several alternatives for how your responsibilities will be handled while you are not on the job, along with your recommendation of the best one. (Note: do not put these into place without prior agreement from your manager.)

6. Identify and quantify any business benefits to the new arrangement.

7. Identify any additional costs or risks to the business, and devise a mitigation plan.

Sometimes it is easier to gain understanding if you share the reason for the change with your manager beforehand: return to work after maternity, caring for a sick relative, or some other reason.

Here is how the conversation might start:

"As you know, I am now returning to work after maternity leave, and I would like to get your feedback on an alternative work arrangement. I would like to work an 80% schedule: Monday through Thursday.

"I know there is a policy of allowing for this, but I am concerned about how to ensure that all of my clients are properly served.

"I have thought about it, and have some ideas for addressing the concern…

"I would like to open the discussion early enough so that if we have to make any changes, there is ample time; what are your thoughts?"

Probably the most important factor in getting buy-in is to indicate a degree of flexibility: if important meetings require your attendance, you won't have a problem shifting your personal schedule to accommodate.

For organizations where your desired alternative work arrangement has never been tried before, recognize the possibility that you may not be able to reach an accommodation. If a non-traditional work arrangement is that important to you, you may have to look for a job elsewhere to get it. This is the primary reason that your homework (especially points 2 and 4 above) are so important.

I Am Thinking of Leaving – What Will You Do to Keep Me?

This is the conversation that should never take place, because it appears to be an ultimatum: if you don't give me what I want, then I will quit! When you deliver this bomb, you may be putting your manager into an instant crisis mode. They may go to their manager for advice and guidance. What could that advice be?

- *"Let the ungrateful lout go: since they don't care about the firm, then the firm shouldn't care about them."*

- *"It probably is a bluff, let's play it out. If they leave, too bad. If they stay, it will be on our terms."*

It is far more productive to have the discussions along the way, so that there is no surprise. Don't put yourself (and your manager) into a lose-lose situation.

But what if you are now really thinking of leaving, and you want to give your current employer one last chance to come up with a set of interesting options?

Ultimatums win you no friends and get you no support.

Remember, career planning is all about you defining what is of interest to you, and then filling in the gaps until you become qualified for that next role. Expecting your employer to provide suggestions is abdicating your personal responsibility for your career. How does your employer know what is best for you? You've again put them in a no-win situation: since they can't possibly know what's best for you, any suggestion they make will likely be rejected by you.

A far better approach would be to discuss your career goals much earlier in the process, without the pressure – or threat – of departure. Consider this conversation with your manager. Of course, you would book an appointment, so you can have the manager's undivided attention.

"I've started to think about the different career paths that I can take, and I've realized that I don't know about all of the options that are available to me. Should I stay with my present group? Change to a different field or specialty? International transfers? Secondment to a client?

"I wanted to meet with you to learn – or find out how I can learn – about these options. At the same time, we've worked together for a number of years, and I would value your perspective on where my strengths lie.

"Ultimately, I would like to lay the groundwork for the next step in my career, and I realize that I can't do it alone. For example, should I enrol for another professional designation – and if so, which one? Would it be possible to be assigned certain types of tasks, so that I can develop experience in that area?

"I've developed a draft Career Commitment Chart that outlines some of my personal career objectives, and the activities that I think will help me achieve them. What do you think...?"

The goal is to engage the experience of those around you to help you achieve your goals. Replay the above conversation, and note that the responsibility for your career stays where it should: with you. (It never gets delegated back to your employer.)

I Am Leaving

Telling your current employer that you will be leaving can be exciting and scary. After all, you have spent many happy productive years there, and leaving, even for a great new position, is bittersweet.

How will the news be taken by those you tell? Your good news is very likely their bad news. Your manager, who is faced with the prospect of replacing an invaluable employee, might feel as if you were leaving them in the lurch. Your mentors within the organization might feel that your leaving is a repudiation of all their advice, and possibly a betrayal of their trust – especially if you haven't confided in them beforehand. And your staff will also feel great uncertainty.

Remember that all these people are not privy to the thinking and analysis that you have done to get yourself to this point. Consider the following conversation, possibly with your manager:

"I've done some hard thinking about where my career is taking me, and what should be next. I've looked at some of my life priorities and have had to make a number of tough decisions. How much time to spend with my older parents? How much time to spend with my younger children? How much time traveling? What might my next position actually be?

"As a result, I am now looking at doing XYZ next. I have looked at the question of how, and have a plan to achieve this goal...

"I've had an excellent run here at ABCD Co., and the experience gained is what has in fact led to my decision to go. I will miss everyone, but am hoping that we might still find a way to do business together...

"Thank you very much for all you have taught me. I will miss our working relationship...

"I'm looking to leave within the month. I've got some ideas on how to ensure an orderly transition, and if you like, we can discuss...

"Here is my letter of resignation..."

One of the most important goals of this discussion is to leave on good terms. No matter what your personal feelings are, remember that it is a small world indeed. Any ill will that you create upon your departure will blemish all you have accomplished, and will tarnish your reputation for years.

It is best to be professional, and honestly try to empathize with the feelings of the person you are telling. If your ego makes this especially hard for you, imagine that you will have to call them up the next day in your new role and sell them something. Don't burn your bridges. Convey that you are moving to what is next for you and not running away from them.

You must have agreement with your employer on the timing of your departure, and how they want your time spent until you leave. Is it working on a special project? Documenting your current responsibilities? Working on a transition plan? Or do they wish to walk you out the door immediately? You may have already developed a succession or transition plan, which now only need be implemented.

Leave on good terms: you never know when you'll next need their goodwill.

You must also gain agreement on how your departure will be communicated. Think about offering to write your departure communiqué, to be sent over your manager's signature. Your colleagues must be told, as must your clients and (if you deal with them) your suppliers. Rather than take your chances with a message that might not be to your liking, agree on the protocol for letting each group know. At the same time, you must be careful to avoid soliciting (and the appearance of soliciting) soon-to-be former clients.

Leaving on good terms is important for another reason:. what if you become a returnee? Or what if a merger places you there? Several years ago, a new employee joined my group after leaving a competitor. It seems his departure was not on the best of terms; in fact, we often heard him deriding his former colleagues. Lo and behold, there was a merger of our parent organizations, and his old group and the current group suddenly became "one." He found himself face to face with his former spurned bosses. He didn't last long.

In the same way that your manager must be left with the appropriate message, so must your mentors, your staff, and colleagues.

"INTERNAL" MENTORS: You may have included your mentor(s) in your Reality Check Interviews, in which case they know that something may be cooking. Even if you didn't interview them, your relationship may be strong enough that you have already told them anyway. No matter which, it would be wise to alert your mentors first, before you speak to your manager. They may have a perspective that you hadn't considered. Or they may suggest another opportunity within the organization that you hadn't even known about. After you speak to them, your final decision to leave might not be so final after all.

Keep your mentors in the loop.

On the other hand, you must consider the risk that your mentor may share your comments with your manager (and others) prematurely. And when your manager finds out, they may not hear about the reasons or your willingness to help during the transition. They will only hear that a bomb will soon be dropped; they will take steps to protect the enterprise, but end up hurting you.

STAFF AND COLLEAGUES: It is important to speak to your closest staff, including those whom you mentor, in person, and as soon as possible after you speak to your manager. It is a judgment call as to whether you tell your closest confidantes beforehand. I have done so, but not without risk.

The message for your staff is that your reason for departure relates to your personal goals; it is not about the company and it is certainly not about them. The second message is that there is as much opportunity after your departure as before, and that you are but a phone call away if they need to contact you. You want to let them know how your time will be filled until your departure, and that a transition plan is being worked on.

After a number of years building part of a business, a common question is what will happen to your group (and your clients) after you leave. Will your contributions endure? Will you be remembered positively? Your staff and colleagues play a key role after you leave: they help preserve your legacy. Making sure that your group continues functioning upon your departure is one way to ensure that the momentum you built continues.

It is in your strongest interest to be remembered by your colleagues, staff, mentors, and managers as a professional, someone with whom they would work again, and whose departure is happening on good terms.

You've Just Been Fired

There are many reasons for why you may be fired. And the vast majority of these reasons are completely beyond your control. While it is beyond the scope of this book to go through all the complexities, if this has happened to you (or if you are worried about it), here is some basic advice:

Be prepared: this means taking responsibility for your career by continuing to invest in yourself: education, networking, and the other concepts discussed in this book. Not only will this make you more valuable to prospective employers, it will make you more valuable to your current one too.

If you are let go (under any circumstance), remember to spend more time listening than anything else. This is exceptionally difficult, as the emotions of the situation will be intensive. The biggest risk is that you may say something that you will later regret, either in the ensuing months or later in your career. Secondly, most employment lawyers will tell you that you shouldn't sign any papers while you are in a state of emotional duress. Take the paperwork, take your notes, and consider what has happened. Depending on the jurisdiction, and depending on any employment contract you have signed, your rights may vary greatly. Understanding your options is a fairly high priority.

At this time, you will likely be concerned about a number of issues. At the top of the list will be how to meet your financial obligations, what to tell friends and family, how the change will be communicated to your colleagues and clients, and of course, how will you find your next job. To address these (and other) questions, write them down, and deal with them logically one by one. Most employers provide outplacement services to ex-employees immediately upon dismissal; your career counselor can help you work through some of these details.

It may come as a surprise to you, but your employer has a worry list as well: how to keep your colleagues motivated (e.g., will I be next?), what to say to your clients (e.g., will there be disruption?), and how to make sure that you will remain "friendly" to the firm as an alumni (and therefore refer new clients). Both you and your employer have very strong incentives to make the parting amicable.

It may come as a surprise, but your employer has a worry list as well.

In my firm, when I laid off one of my earliest employees, she was stunned. She had outgrown her role and had tremendous potential, but at the time my company didn't have a place for her to spread her wings. While it wouldn't have been exactly right for me to tell her that she would thank me in a year's time, we parted amicably, and after a year, she did indeed thank me. Sometimes, we all stay in jobs a bit too long, and our employers are the ones who have to tell us that it is time for a change.

While it may be the last thing on your mind, visualize some time in the future when you are applying for a job, and will need the person who fired you as a reference. Or a few years later, imagine that this person is the hiring manager for a hot job you would love to get. Career Insight: despite the personal satisfaction it may bring, don't burn your bridges.

FOCUS

- Talking to your manager – and earning their support – is a critical step in the career development process.

- Change is difficult and takes people by surprise. Make sure that you prepare them beforehand; make them party to the transition.

- Always keep your mentors in the loop.

- If you leave for any reason, do so on friendly terms: you will see your former colleagues, and need your former colleagues, throughout your entire career.

ACTION CHECKLIST

❏ Discuss your Career Commitment Chart with your manager to elicit their feedback and support.

❏ Continue to expand your education, experience, and network no matter what your career goals are.

Chapter 17:
Networking

CHAPTER IN A FLASH: *Networking is a core skill for both business development and any job search. Add value by remembering Give to Get: Growing your network by Giving; this chapter describes precisely how to do it.*

Over the last ten years a tremendous degree of research has been undertaken on the science of networking. You may have heard the term *six degrees of separation*, which suggests that anyone can connect to anyone else by speaking to a friend, who knows a friend, who knows a friend, who knows a friend, who knows a friend, who knows the target. While a cute concept, a more important one for us is *two degrees of separation*. Whether you are looking for a job or looking for more business, the question isn't who you know, but who your friends know. The stronger the relationships you have with your friends, the more they will be on the lookout for jobs – or business – that can help you. Where do they get the leads? From their friends – the second degree of separation.

Networking has a simple goal: developing and strengthening relationships.

Consider yourself: how many people do you know? What is the strength of those relationships? Think about your graduating class – how many could you call on the telephone and have a decent conversation with, let alone have them remember your name without prompting? If you are like most people, you remember those who have meaning to you (both personal and professional). Those whom you have little time for – well, you have little time for them, and the relationship lapses. This is one degree of separation. If the relationship is so weak that they barely remember your name, what is the probability that they will let you tap their networks? There is no *two degrees of separation* in this case.

Your network is a long-term asset that grows more valuable over time. It can provide insight into different options, and it can help with the Reality Check Interview process. As it develops, your network is even more precious. It can provide career options, business leads, introductions to prospective clients, valuable business advice, and much-needed personal support.

For most younger professionals, networking is measured by the number of business cards collected. Usually the stack of cards sits next to the computer for several weeks; you then contemplate both your new "relationships" and your guilt about doing nothing with the cards. If you have time, you load the information into your computer. If you don't have time, you eventually shuffle the cards to a back drawer. In both cases, you don't have a relationship, and therefore you don't have a network.

Networking has a simple goal: to move the other party up the *relationship curve* from awareness, to preference, to commitment. The higher they are on the curve, the more both parties will benefit.

Let's not make networking any more difficult than it has to be. Most people are very familiar with the first part of the networking process: *Fish where the fish are*. Many people are very familiar (and very uncomfortable) with the second part of the networking process: *Meeting new people*. Most people never even consider the most critical task of networking: *Give to Get: Growing your network by Giving*.

Fish Where the Fish Are

The first step is to put yourself in a position to meet new people. This means getting out from behind your computer and attending events where other people will be: in other words, fish where the fish are. What you will find is that many other attendees are there primarily for networking as well. And they may also be as uncomfortable doing it as you are. The number of venues for networking is limitless, but here is a short list to get you started:

- Attending trade association meetings or business conferences.
- Joining any community group at any level.
- Attending professional development seminars.
- Participating at an athletic/fitness club.
- Attending your firm's receptions and events.
- Attending alumni events from your university or college.
- Joining a networking or mastermind group.
- Joining a board of directors.
- Attending cultural events (symphony, ballet, opera, art gallery openings, etc.)
- Participating at interactive events (wine tasting, bridge clubs, hiking groups, etc.)
- Attending sports events.

Meeting New People

It is simple human nature to gravitate to the familiar and avoid the uncomfortable. In a networking environment, we do this by seeking out those we already know and spending time with them. Try to resist this temptation. Instead, touch base quickly with those you already know, and then meet new people. As you get each person's business card, speak to them long enough to learn three specific things that they are interested in, either personally or professionally. When you have done so, politely excuse yourself with a promise to touch base later (don't forget to do that!). Then write down these three interests on the back of their card.

This is the second step to successfully networking: it is not schmoozing, nor is it fluff conversations about the weather – your mission is to introduce yourself and collect information. Finally, repeat the process with another person. When you get home, you'll still have a stack of cards, but at least you'll know something about each person's interests.

The Bank of ME

One of the most asked questions is how to get an informational interview. (Informational interviews are designed to help you learn about an industry, an organization, or a job function.) Consider what these interviews really are, but from the perspective of the other party: somewhere between a waste of time and... a waste of time. Why, other than for reasons of charity or pity, would someone who barely knows you agree to this type of interview? Yet they happen, and they are a key part of the career development process. It is true that there are some big-hearted people who remember what it was like doing the "job search thing." They agree to meet you because they see it as a way to pay back for their current success; unfortunately, they are in the minority.

You can't make a withdrawal without first making a deposit.

Most bankers will tell you that if you would like to make a withdrawal, you need to first make a deposit. If there is no money in the account, you can't make a withdrawal. (For the time being, we'll put aside such things as overdraft protection.) If you have not made a "deposit" with the person you are hoping to ask, you won't be able to make a withdrawal. In other words, unless you can create a degree of obligation, don't bother asking for help – you'll look like a job beggar.

Of course, if you haven't created that obligation yourself, you can borrow someone else's: have a friend request a meeting on your behalf –

two degrees of separation. Even this isn't a free ride: you have now created a debt to your friend. We'll look at how to pay them back and create more – *Give to Get* – later in this chapter.

Defining Your Existing Network: The Networking Name List

How do you measure the strength of your network? Consider the following exercise, taken from the insurance industry but very applicable here. New recruits are asked to identify their natural market – that is, those whom they have a relationship with. The exercise – to create a Networking Name List – is simple. Write down 150 people whom you have a relationship with, and then rank how each person sees *their relationship with you* – either good, neutral, bad, or lapsed. Consider categorizing this list, perhaps by how you met each person (college, former supplier, family relation, etc.) If you can write down 150 names easily, keep adding 25 people until you honestly cannot write down any more. If you are having trouble coming up with 150 names, write down as many as you can, then push yourself to find another 25.

Were you surprised by how many (or how few) people were on your list? Were you a bit embarrassed about how many relationships were lapsed? Developing and keeping relationships is not only for those who are natural at schmoozing. It is a learned skill that can be done in a number of different ways. Whole books have been written on the subject, but I want to suggest a practical system, modified from a process taught to me by one of my earlier mentors.

Give to Get: Growing Your Network by Giving

The whole objective of networking is to expand your contact list in two ways: increase the number of relationships and increase the quality of those relationships. Obviously, this cannot continue indefinitely – your time is finite, after all – so the challenge is to keep as many balls in the air as possible, slowly but surely moving each person up the relationship curve.

One of the less well-known capabilities of Microsoft Outlook[4] is the ability to flag a follow-up reminder for a contact. After opening a contact, click on the red "follow-up" flag, and then choose a custom date. Here's how the networking system works:

---

4   Microsoft Outlook is one of the most popular email/calendar/contact management programs; it shouldn't be confused with Microsoft's Outlook Express, a different, far more limited program. While the instructions given in this section are specific to Outlook, they can be adapted to the many other contact management programs that are available.

1. The beginning part of every day is spent "processing" your follow-ups.

2. For each follow-up contact, send them something in the postal mail, or send them something via email, or leave them a voice message about something, or call them about something. Note that in each case, you are *giving*, not *taking*: you are making a deposit in the bank of ME.

   What is the "something" that you send them? That depends on their interests – which is why you wrote these down on the back of their business cards. Here are some examples of things that you can give:

   - Subscribe to a number of business magazines. As you are scanning each issue, tear out articles that might be of interest to people in your network and send those articles out to them. Rather than spending the time writing a letter, staple your business card to the article, and write a brief "FYI"-type note directly on the card.

   - Take a relevant link from a web site that they wouldn't see themselves and send it via email. Make sure that it isn't to a password-protected site: they won't be able to see what you send them!

   - Electronically send them a white paper that you wrote.

   - Send them a birthday or similar "congratulations" card.

   - Leave them a voice message pointing them to something relevant, without creating the obligation for them to return your call.

   - Call them about getting together for breakfast, lunch, a sporting event, or something similar, to reconnect.

   - Call them to offer "extra" tickets for a sporting event or a symphony performance.

   - There is no limit to what you can do; it's limited only by how much you know about their interests.

   Important: Never, ever, send something that looks like a form letter. Never, ever, send email "bulk" to a number of people at once, either visibly with cc's, or invisibly with bcc's. Each one must look, and be, completely personal and individualized.

3. After sending the item out or making the phone call, record the event (date and what was sent or said) in the contact notes area in Outlook; then set the next follow-up date. Depending on how strong the relationship is, set the follow-up date to 12 months, 3 months, 6 weeks,

or as low as 4 weeks. In rare cases, you might want to remove someone completely from the follow-up schedule. Clearly, the stronger the relationship, the faster the cycle the person would be on.

4. How to start: If they aren't there already, add each of the 150 "natural market" contacts into your Outlook Contact list. Then fish those business cards from the back of your drawer (from previous networking events), and try to remember just one thing about each contact that will give you a clue as to what they might be interested in. Now go through the list one by one, and set follow-up dates. Try to spread out the initial follow-up dates so that you don't have a big "lump" of work to do when that date comes around. If you have an excessive number of contacts, start with your highest priority contacts first.

Using a regular process to reach out to your contacts guarantees stronger relationsihps.

How many contacts might this work for? On average if your contacts are on a three-month rotation (i.e., 60 business days), and you "send out" 15 things each day, then you can manage a network 900 people strong. This is far more than the 150 names we discussed earlier in the chapter! The math is actually quite alluring: if you send or call only three contacts daily, an exceptionally low number, with an average three-month rotation, you can manage a 180-person network.

The system helps keep the relationship alive through the value that you add; when you need their help, or when they need yours, the relationship investment will pay off. As you rise through the ranks, relationship management and business development will become your most critical skills. You will realize that these two effectively are the same thing: the stronger the relationship, the more you have become their advisor of choice. Later, in the chapter on Business Development, we will expand on this concept significantly.

FOCUS

- Your network is a compounding investment: each year it develops more critical mass and becomes more valuable.

- The essence of networking isn't small talk or collecting business cards: it is Give to Get – The more you give, the more you get back.

- Developing relationships is a hands-on activity, but to be successful with it requires process.

ACTION CHECKLIST

❏ Develop your Networking Name List.

❏ Find time each day for Give to Get. Even if you start small, start making deposits in the bank of ME.

Chapter 18:
Notes for Entrepreneurs

CHAPTER IN A FLASH: *Creating a business plan organizes all of your ideas and helps you better articulate them to others. Get help when you start: legal, accounting, and a corporate identity.*

If you are one of the brave souls looking to start your own business, then writing a traditional business plan is a must. How widely you share the plan will depend on your chosen option. In some cases, it means using the plan to present to investors; in other cases, it may mean showing it only to a few close confidantes. While there are many books (and online resources) that can help you to write your plan, the basic outline should address the following topics:

BUSINESS DESCRIPTION AND STRATEGY: What is the business's purpose, and how will it be achieved? What is the business model? How is the strategy unique and sustainable?

FINANCIAL: What is the ownership structure? Where is the money coming from, and where will it be spent? You will need to include three years of financial projections and sensitivity analysis, along with supporting assumptions.

MARKETING: Describe the marketing processes, including branding, partnerships, advertising, direct mail, Internet. Who are the competitors, and how is the enterprise differentiated?

SALES: Describe the sales channels, strategies, and the sales process. Describe any existing "pipeline" and the assumptions supporting the sales forecast.

> Writing a business plan will make it easier to sell your ideas to others.

OPERATIONS: Describe how the product is produced, inventoried, and shipped. If you will be providing a service, describe the methodology. Describe R&D plans, including any unique intellectual property.

HR: Include mini-bios of all key executives. Describe unique HR policies and plans. Describe your role in detail.

Many other sections can be added to a business plan, depending on the situation. Feel free to be creative, but do spend the time putting at least something down on paper, no matter what your chosen option. Writing it down gives you, yet again, the opportunity to fine-tune your decision.

Finally, rehearse your business plan presentation in front of a number of friendly faces. This will help you become more comfortable with your new vocabulary, and the feedback will help you build confidence.

Professional Services

BOOKKEEPING AND ACCOUNTING: From the very start of your efforts, you will likely be incurring *bona fide* expenses. Some costs might be those related to your home office, others might be for professional services (e.g., legal and accounting), while others might be related to marketing and sales.

Before engaging a lawyer or accountant, write down all of your questions.

You will need to define a mechanism to capture these expenses as they are being incurred. At the same time, you will need to determine what computer software to use, set up a chart of accounts, and decide whether you should do the bookkeeping yourself or outsource it.

LEGAL ADVICE: When you visit a bookstore, you will be amazed at the number of books that provide pseudo-legal advice: from incorporating your own company, to providing "standard" contract forms, to filing trademarks, to filing lawsuits. If you are even thinking of relying on these generalized how-to guides for your legal needs, don't. These guides might not take into account the specifics of common law in your jurisdiction. They might not be up to date. And they certainly don't take into account anything particular about your situation. The bookstore guides can be useful, though, for a different reason: you will learn the lingo – which should help you advise your legal counsel more effectively.

Dealing with professionals must be done in as efficient a manner as possible, or else fees will become an issue. One way of enhancing efficiency is to ensure that they are focused on providing legal advice. This means providing your lawyer with a "term sheet" that should form the basis of a contract, rather than having your lawyer (and the counterparty's lawyer) haggle over business terms. Of course, some lawyers provide business advisory services as well, often assisting in business negotiation. If this is how you are using your lawyer, no problem, but be aware that this is what you are doing. Another possibility is to ask your lawyer to write template contracts (e.g., employment contracts, confidentiality agreements, vendor agreements). Too many businesses write new contracts for each deal they do.

Corporate Identity

Developing a brand and an identity is important for all businesses. Presumably, you already have a business name and have now secured (and protected) your rights to use it. Instead of spending money at the local photocopy shop getting generic business cards and stationery, engage a professional graphic designer to develop your corporate identity. This may include a logo, stationery, and business cards.

If the designer has experience, they will also be able to design your PowerPoint presentation template and a simple web site. (The web site can always be enhanced once you have your enterprise under way.) These simple investments, which you will have to make anyway, lend important credibility, especially at the beginning.

One young entrepreneur, selling his services to a multinational, had his business cards printed with the title "Sales Manager." Asked why he did this, rather than having the title of "President" or "Managing Director," he responded that having a less senior title meant that his customers would assume there was significant infrastructure behind him. And, he continued, since he looked so young, having a senior title would give him less credibility than a junior one. For him, developing a personal brand that was fully congruent was critical to his sales efforts. Chapter 20 develops this theme further. Whether this anecdote applies in your situation or not, it illustrates the importance of attention to detail when it comes to your identity and its impact.

FOCUS

- The value in committing your business plan to paper is that you will have to think through it thoroughly first.

ACTION CHECKLIST

❏ Write out your Business Plan, and get feedback on it.
❏ Get specialized help for non-core activities.

Chapter 19:
If You Are Going to Leave

CHAPTER IN A FLASH: *Know your rights and obligations, but if you leave, make sure that you do so on good terms.*

If you do decide to leave your current employer, all your attention should be on the new opportunity itself. Don't be distracted by logistics and administration.

Your Rights and Obligations

When you started your current job, you may have signed an employment agreement that imposed specific obligations on you and your employer. An employment agreement, however, is not the only place that rights and obligations are defined. For example, obligations may be embedded in an employment application that you signed years ago, or in confidentiality agreements that you sign annually. You may implicitly agree to other obligations (and give up certain rights) when you log on to an email system or intranet. Obligations are also derived from employment law.

This law varies by jurisdiction. At one extreme, many American states have *employment at will* laws, by which employees can quit (or be fired) with no notice, obligation, or special payment. At the other extreme, some Canadian provinces and some European countries are slanted so far in the employees' favor that it is almost impossible to fire an employee, except at great cost. Often, the statute law mandates certain minimums with respect to severance, notice, and employment conditions. Common law (i.e., the body of law derived from court rulings) usually extends legislation considerably.

Whether because of the law, your company's policies, or an explicit employment agreement, you should clarify a number of areas before you leave. Since every situation is unique, make sure to hire legal counsel to advise you on the specifics of your circumstances.

SEVERANCE: If you leave on your own accord, what severance, if any, is payable?

NOTICE: How much notice must you give your employer, according to the letter of your agreement? If your agreement is silent on this, what is the minimum length of notice you are required to give, by law? What is the length of notice you *should* give to allow an orderly transfer of responsibility and to maintain a friendly relationship? Can you give notice at any time of the year, or is there a particular time when you must give notice (e.g., 30 days prior to a contract anniversary or at the end of a project)? Note that there is a difference between the legal obligations (which you need to resolve) and the "right thing to do." Many individuals will return to their former employers either as employees, clients, or suppliers; the less disruptive your change can be, the higher your credibility will remain.

NON-COMPETE: Are you restricted from competing with your employer in any way? Be sure to get legal advice if you have restrictions and if your next role might be considered competition.

NON-SOLICITATION: Once you leave, are you restricted in any way from contacting or soliciting current or past customers? Are you restricted in any way from hiring (or even providing a reference for) your former colleagues?

INTELLECTUAL PROPERTY RIGHTS: Have you given to your current employer any and all intellectual property rights to everything you were involved in while employed? Or did you retain some degree of ownership? If you developed a process or methodology while with your current employer, could you use the same process with your new employer? Do you have any right to keep any of your correspondence and files? Most will not, but if you do, when you do move to your new position, what steps must you take to make sure you are not sued for intellectual property infringement?

Understand your legal and contractual position.

REIMBURSED EXPENSES AND ACCRUALS: At what point can the company stop paying your expenses: at the time of notice, your last day on the job, or at some later time? Medical bills or insurance fees, for example, may come due after you have left, but may relate to services performed while you are an employee. You may find that certain benefits (such as life or disability insurance) may continue for a period of time beyond the termination of your employment. Pay particular attention to any vacation accruals you have earned over your entire career with your employer.

TIMING ISSUES AND THE COST OF LEAVING: Depending on when (and how) you leave, what happens to your stock options, warrants, restricted stock, or other equity participation? Do you lose anything that is not yet vested? Do you have a certain amount of time to exercise any vested options or warrants after you've departed, or do they all expire immediately? Make sure that you see a copy of the policy in writing, prior to making any final decisions. A question answered verbally by someone without the authority to answer could cost you dearly if they are wrong.

Similarly, there is an issue of the status of commissions, bonuses, deferred compensation, and pension benefits. It would be worthwhile to understand your employer's policy and practice in these areas.

CLAW-BACKS: Are there any expenses (clubs memberships, medical expenses, conference fees, training expenses, etc.) that the organization will expect you to pay back on your leaving, either in full or *pro rata*? Often this is a bit of a surprise, as one's final pay may be substantially lower (or negative!) as a result of these obligations.

Benefits

Evaluate your entire benefits package for portability. For example, life insurance can often be purchased by an employee on termination of employment without evidence of good health, so long as it is done within a set period of time. If you have a health problem, you may not be able to get life insurance privately or at your new position. If this is the case, buying out your current group policy, at any cost, may be worthwhile. Before you do it, though, review your entire insurance plan with a trusted insurance professional.

FOCUS

- If you are going to leave, do whatever you can to leave on good terms with your reputation intact.

ACTION CHECKLIST

❑ Review your rights and obligations; evaluate changes in benefits.

Chapter 20:
Job Search Skills

CHAPTER IN A FLASH: *Searching for a job is a process with a number of discrete parts. Personal Branding is a synthesis between what people see, what you do, and what you represent. An Elevator Pitch – a short description of yourself – must be framed in terms that are relevant to the listener. Each phrase within your resumé must have a story attached to it. There are a number of different interview styles – make sure you know what to expect.*

After earning her credentials, a young manager took a corporate position. After 16 years and many promotions, she was called into her manager's office where she was told that she no longer had a job. Unfortunately, this scenario is played out in every type of organization, every day of the year. Whether the reason is changing business requirements, political issues, or something else, it is a shock to the system. If she were prepared, some of the shock could have been avoided.

There is a secret to job search – a big one. Most people already know it implicitly, but here it is written in full:

The Key Success Factors for your current job are the same ones that will qualify you for a job if you don't have one. These include such basics as attitude, education and training, networking, and filling in the gaps.

The corollary to this is simple: if you do none of these things while you are employed, expect to spend your valuable time ramping up if you find yourself unemployed. And even more bluntly: if you do none of these things while you are employed, perhaps it shouldn't be a surprise if you find yourself unemployed.

And the positive flip-side: if you are filling in the gaps in order to leave, you may find that your added value will translate into greater opportunities where you are now.

CAREER PLANNING INSIGHT: Career development activities are critical to your success, no matter what your direction. If your career planning focus has (so far) been limited to scanning through this book instead of working through the frameworks, you might consider going back to start the process in earnest: SkillChecks, Reality Check Interviews, Job Quality Checklist, Personal Balance Sheet, etc.

—⟫·◇·⟪—

While it is beyond the scope of this book to delve deeply into job search strategy, there are parts to a job search that are intimately linked to the concepts described.

The job search process uses certain collaterals (cover letters, resumés, etc.) and requires the development of certain skills (interviewing, networking, etc.). Underlying all of this is the concept of your Personal Brand.

Personal Branding

What type of car do you drive? What brand of clothing do you buy? Many of our purchase decisions are based on the brand: the emotional connection we have with the underlying attributes of these products. Another example: think of Volvo, Cadillac, and Porsche. All three sell models that are sports cars, and all three companies make cars in the same price bracket. Yet each is clearly different: one speaks to safety, the other luxury, and one to speed. While it might seem strange to think of ourselves as products, we actually are. And like branded products, we relay our "brand" outwards: to our friends, family, colleagues – and prospective employers.

A useful way to look at this is my Personal Branding Model. It is divided into three parts: *What they see*, *What you do*, and *What you represent*. The heart of your brand can be found in *what you represent*: you might be "known" as hardworking, analytical, and reliable. Where brands fall apart is when *What they see* and *What you do* send different messages than *What you represent*. If you feel that you are not being recognized for your contributions, or if you are going through job interviews and not having much luck, a contradictory or diffuse personal brand may be the problem.

Personal Branding Model

What They See
- Your clothing
- How you speak/what you say
- Your friendliness
- Your business cards and web site(s)
- The professional look of your resumé/cover letter
- The logic of your resumé/cover letter

What You Do
- Your punctuality
- Your results
- Business knowledge/current events
- Work and life experience
- The intellectual depth of your writing
- Community involvement

What You Represent
- Honest
- Strong work ethic
- Analytical and logical
- Creative out of the box thinker
- Sales dynamo

Expert marketers will tell you that the strongest brands are those that are consistent, congruent, and focused. The diagram describes the levers that are available to you within the model. Check yourself: is your personal brand internally consistent, and are you currently broadcasting the right message?

While they might not use these exact words, companies look for employees whose Personal Brands synchronize with their own. Said another way, you will do well in an organization whose brand – whose culture – complements your own.

Elevator Pitch

Imagine you are going to an interview, you walk into the elevator, and the person recognizes that they will be meeting with you imminently. They say, "Tell me about yourself": you have about a minute of their undivided, exclusive attention in which to say something. At this point, you will either disqualify yourself or pique the listener's interest enough to put a big green checkmark beside your name.

Elevator pitches must be relevant to the listener.

The truth is that prospective employers really don't care about you as an individual: how can they – they don't even know you! All they really care about is how you can solve their problems. So instead of talking about yourself, your elevator pitch must describe yourself in terms that are relevant to the prospective employer. To this end:

- Your elevator pitch must be framed in terms that are benefits to the listener.
- Importance of research! If you don't know the issues, how will you know what to say?
- Your pitch must be grounded in – and congruent with – your personal brand.
- Convey some emotion or passion – but don't overdo it!

Consider these two examples. Which might be more interesting to the listener?

Randall Craig, President of Pinetree Advisors. I have an MBA, a CFA, and a Black Belt in Karate. I am a management consultant, author, and professional speaker.

Randall Craig of Pinetree Advisors; I have worked with over 90 major organizations to solve their toughest problems. We help our clients safely land their strategy airplane.

Get it? Both of these contain important information, but the second is more listener-focused.

Elevator pitches are extremely important from a business development perspective as well. A prospective client may ask for a high-level summary of your proposal, your organization, or your background.

Probably the least sincere elevator pitches are the ones that are memorized. While rehearsal is required, the goal is for it to sound natural – and be authentic. Since the root of the pitch comes from your Personal Brand, there is no reason it shouldn't be.

Resumé

Your resumé has two main purposes: to qualify you for an interview, and to provide material to talk about during the interview itself. In a sense, your resumé is your brand's brochure: your "product attributes" must be relevant to your target audience. Typically, a resumé is a listing of the impacts you have made. It contains bullets with quantified, relevant accomplishments. And it lets the reader understand that you are a person who is capable of leading, managing, directing, and sometimes merely coordinating.

From a career planning perspective, the resumé holds a slightly different role. If someone is reviewing your resumé, they should see a logical, well laid-out story that starts with your background, moves forward through your jobs (each one tightly linking to the next), and whose logical outcome is that you are the perfect candidate for the position in question.

If you are passed over for promotion, or don't get the job, it could mean several things:

1. Your resumé doesn't properly reflect your skills.

2. Your resumé doesn't tell a coherent (and relevant) story.

3. You are not qualified (which is evidence of not filling in the gaps properly).

4. There were better qualified candidates.

To start the resumé writing process itself, pick up a few of the *most recent* books (such as my book, *The Working Resumé)* and go through them.

And finally, a request from all of the HR managers across the country. Please, please, do not use "resume.doc" as the filename for any resumé sent in electronically. You have your own name; there is no reason why you can't use it.

Interviews

For many people, practicing interviews has always been about repeating memorized answers to expected questions. If you answered the questions properly, you were asked back for another interview. Interview preparation was relatively simple: memorize responses based on your experience.

While this approach may have worked several years ago, it is insufficient in today's competitive environment. For one thing, this old approach is all about you – and not about them.

Recall that recruiters and hiring managers really don't care about you. They only care about whether you are able to solve their problems. Therefore, if you don't know their problem, how can you share your experience solving it? You can't. Spend research time identifying the specific problem you're being hired to solve. The problem can be as simple as managing the benefits function, filling a regional sales quota, or coordinating a public filing.

> When you are chosen for an interview, the recruiter is hoping that you will not disqualify yourself by saying something stupid.

Today, the whole interview process is focused on finding out whether you are or are not a *problem solver*. In fact, most experienced interviewers know that if you successfully went through the pre-screening, you might indeed be "the one." Their fervent hope is that you do not disqualify yourself during the interview itself. Many people do.

Of course, sometimes candidates disqualify themselves because they shouldn't have been interviewed in the first place: they weren't properly qualified. Sometimes they disqualify themselves because of nervousness. And sometimes they disqualify themselves because they haven't done adequate preparation. Many times, however, it is because candidates are not well-versed in the variety and styles of the job interview itself.

These newer interview techniques are designed precisely to help expose a candidate's capabilities:

BEHAVIORAL INTERVIEW: This is the "standard" interview that asks you to describe issues based on your resumé and asks how you would handle different hypothetical situations. The trend has been to have more structured interviews, to ensure that each candidate is being evaluated on similar criteria.

STRESS INTERVIEW: Thankfully not used too often, this type of interview has several interviewers peppering you with tough questions, to determine how you cope under pressure.

PANEL INTERVIEW: The traditional panel interview has you sitting across from several interviewers, often answering their questions in sequence.

Sometimes Panels can be Stress Interviews, but inducing stress isn't the primary objective of the Panel. This type of interview is a time-efficient way for several people to assess performance in a formalized setting, often using scoring sheets. A panel is challenging for the candidate, as the interview itself is less of a conversation than an evaluation.

CASE INTERVIEWS: These are becoming more and more common; there are a number of different types:

a. Situational cases: The interviewer gives you a business problem, and you have to answer it by asking questions of them, as if you were a consultant. Example case: *For the first time ever, last month your restaurant lost money. What's going on?* You must ask the right questions to determine the problem, and then recommend the best solution. Your answer should follow a defined framework: Role, Analysis, Alternatives, Recommendation, Action Plan.

Ask about the type of interview beforehand.

Situational cases are excellent because they allow the interviewer to evaluate so many things:

- Your logic and analytical ability (e.g., do the questions asked make sense? Are the conclusions drawn logical?)
- Your creative ability (Are the recommendations innovative?)
- Your business acumen (How quickly can you arrive at your conclusion?)
- Your confidence (Did you convey a sense of knowledge and gravitas, or were you tentative and not credible?)

b. Creativity cases: These cases ask you to brainstorm in a unique way, to assess how flexible your thought processes are. Example case: *If you were a cell phone company, how might you market cars?*

c. Estimation cases: These ask you to determine the market size. Example case: *How big is the skateboard market in China?* In this case, they are measuring your analytical ability.

d. Analysis and Presentation cases: In this type of interview, you are given prep time and a voluminous written case – perhaps 40 pages – then are asked to "solve" it and present your solution to the interviewers. The goal in this type of interview is to assess your ability to separate important information from the rest. Of course, if your analysis isn't up to par, then out you go. And if you cannot present to the group at a strong enough level, out you go as well.

EXPERIENTIAL INTERVIEWS: These are often done in groups and are structured so that the interviewer can observe the team dynamics as the group struggles with the required task. Sometimes the task is to analyze and present a formal business case; sometimes it is to solve a particular type of puzzle.

PHONE INTERVIEWS: These probably should be called pre-screening calls, but more often entire interviews are done over the phone. Partly this is done to allow geographically dispersed managers to participate in the process. The rationale continues: since so many relationships (and so much management) happen long-distance, then having at least one phone interview is an appropriate assessment of your capabilities in the area. Organizations also are doing more phone interviews as they are cheaper, faster and demand fewer logistical arrangements.

Phone interviews are amongst the most challenging, as it impossible to interpret body language without seeing the interviewer. The best you can do is listen closely to their voice, and properly modulate your own.

No matter which interview types you participate in, the most important advice for the prospective candidate is to remain authentic to who you are. If you try to be something that you are not, it will be obvious to the experienced interviewer. If they hire you because of you, the probability of your success is significantly increased. If they hire the *inauthentic you*, you will likely not enjoy the job, nor will you excel in it.

FOCUS

- Your Personal Brand, Elevator Pitch, cover letter, resumé, interview performance (and job performance) all reflect who you are: strive for authenticity and congruency.

- Personal Branding Model: What they see, what you do, what you represent.

- Your Elevator Pitch must be framed in terms that are benefits to the listener.

ACTION CHECKLIST

❏ Create, review, or update your resumé and Elevator Pitch so they are congruent with your Personal Brand.

Chapter 21:
Making the Most of a Mentoring Relationship

CHAPTER IN A FLASH: *Mentoring is a two-way street – you'll get greater value from your mentor if you add value back into the relationship.*

Mentors play a special role in the career development and advancement of most successful people. Mentors can provide valuable advice and perspective on many facets of a career, from handling difficult decisions to smoothing the political way when problems occur. They also act as a role model and, at times, a trusted friend.

But what about the role of the mentee? Relationships are a two-way street; the mentee must add value too: think Give to Get.

1. **DELIVER ON YOUR PROMISES.** It is critical that you keep your promises. Commit to doing something at your mentor's suggestion and deliver to a standard of excellence. When you make a commitment and keep it, not only do you impress the mentor, but you also feel good about yourself. By delivering on your promises, you are telling the mentor that his or her advice is valuable.

2. **RETURN THE FAVOR.** Discover your mentor's "hot buttons." Determine if you can help them solve an issue they may be experiencing. Show interest in what is happening in their world, and lend a hand if you are able.

3. **RETURN THE FAVOR TO OTHERS.** Become a mentor. Take on someone in a more junior capacity as a mentee. They can provide invaluable information to you, as they are now part of your network. Mentoring adds value and helps build self-confidence.

4. **MAINTAIN CONFIDENTIALITY.** Do not broadcast any discussions to colleagues or other people inside or outside the organization. Consider whether the mentoring relationship needs to be discreet to avoid jealous feelings from your colleagues.

5. **KEEP YOUR MENTOR INFORMED.** When acting on the mentor's advice, be sure to circle back to let them know the outcome. It is frustrating for a mentor to give advice and never know what happens.

6. **SHOW APPRECIATION.** A mentor is providing two priceless gifts: their experience and their time. Be grateful for having them in your life, and be sure to thank them with kind words and deeds.

7. **RESPECT THEIR TIME.** Mentors have busy lives, too. If the mentor is not available when advice is needed, use good judgment and do not be a nuisance (e.g., do not interrupt your mentor when they are on vacation).

8. **LEARN FROM THEM.** Whenever a mentor is not accessible, try asking yourself this question: "What would my mentor do?" Asking this question shifts your perspective, and allows you to see the situation with a new light: your mentor's. In fact, the closer your mentoring relationship, the better your answer will be.

ACTION CHECKLIST

❏ Are you a good mentee? For each of your mentors, go through this chapter and determine what you can do to improve your relationships further.

Long-Term Success

Congratulations. Your career plan is bearing fruit. You've been rewarded with new responsibilities or a great promotion. Perhaps you have started your own company. Maybe you have the title "President" on your business card for the first time. Whatever you are now doing, you are expecting greater personal fulfillment, financial rewards, and hopefully, better life balance.

Being successful in your new role has very little to do with luck and very much to do with hard work, having the right attitude, and avoiding silly mistakes.

This part of the book provides perspective, as well as guidance on business relationships, adjusting to change, and extended leaves. And it answers a key question: *How do you start?*

Chapter 22:
Business Development: Cheap, Smart, and Trusted

CHAPTER IN A FLASH: *Developing strong relationships is a key business skill: relationships open the door to new business – and more career opportunities. This philosphy is quite different from one that competes exclusively on price or expertise.*

If you speak to a product marketing expert, sales success is dependent on many factors, first and foremost being the Four Ps: Price, Product, Place, and Promotion. While this is also true when you are selling services, consider the PET model as well: Price, Expertise, and Trust. It answers the question about the basis of your sales and marketing efforts: how do you compete? And in so doing, the model defines the basis of your business relationships. We'll draw a straight line to your career shortly, but for the moment, consider how you (or your organization) use this model.

Tier One: Price

At the most basic level, you are competing on price. The client may see your "package" as being a simple commodity – and therefore the cheaper the better. If you are selling professional services, this is clearly not where you would like to be, as there will always be someone who is willing to shave their margins just that much more, in order to capture market share.

For organizations that compete on price, the mantra is simple: reduce product cost, reduce cost of service delivery, outsource wherever possible, and make it up on volume. (And of course, try to differentiate your product or package away from the other commodities filling this space.)

Tier Two: Expertise

Because it takes longer to acquire, expertise has greater staying power than price. Competing on expertise, particularly for service-based businesses, is the primary mode of differentiation. Every client engagement, every additional course, moves you to guru-hood. Clients will always value specialization and focus; these two items reduce business risk and (by following your advice) help clients differentiate themselves from their competition.

In fact, if you look at most marketing proposals, the greatest amount of space is usually reserved for the section that matches the organization's qualifications against the client's needs.

The problem with an expertise-based strategy is that there will always be others who are that much fresher and that much sharper than you are. And if a client thinks that they are smarter, even if they aren't, the result is the same: out with the old (you), and in with the new.

For organizations that compete on expertise, their mantra is also simple: hire the smartest, invest heavily in professional development, provide challenging work assignments to extend the expertise, then invest in knowledge management systems to make the expertise available on demand to those who need it.

Tier Three: Trust

The third and final tier is that of a trusted advisor. At this level, the client doesn't see you as a vendor or a customer but sees you as an independent, objective professional who will provide perspective on any question. What's your view on the economy? The new export legislation? About switching to that new supplier? A particular accounting treatment? Of course, you cannot provide answers to all these questions, as you are certainly not an expert in all of them. But as a trusted advisor, you have earned the right to be asked. Here is how you might answer these questions:

- "I'm not sure, but why not call Joe Smith at the ABC Company – he's an expert in the area."

- "I'm not the best person to ask, but let me see if I can find someone for you."

- "This is something we've done for XYZ Co.: Do you want to speak to my colleague who did the work there?"

- "Great question: why don't I take a few hours and put together a note for you on it?"

Notice that in only one of these sample answers are you personally taking on the work. If you were competing on expertise, you may have grabbed the work as a great way to develop even wider expertise. Instead, you implicitly told the client that your relationship is worth far more than a few dollars. While the price competitor may lament that money was left on the table, the exact opposite is true: at some point in the future, the person who receives the referral will return the favor to you.

The only viable long-term strategy for those engaged in selling services is to move as quickly as possible to the third tier: becoming the advisor of choice.

Career Implications

If you have been reading this chapter thinking about the organization that you work for, consider the model again at the personal level: what should your personal strategy be? Would you prefer to be known as the cheapest, the smartest, or the most trusted?

This model makes even more sense when you consider the relationships between the tiers. Without delivering value (tier one), you may not even be considered for a particular role. Without delivering expertise (tier two), you may not get close enough to develop a trust relationship. And without developing and delivering trust (tier three), your recommendations will lack credibility and therefore not be implemented. And without implementation, questions arise about your value – which brings us back to tier one!

Think about the entire recruitment process: from the posting of an open position, to the cover letter, resumé, the various interviews, and the reference checks. Is not the whole process designed to assess Price, Expertise, and Trust?

For example, at college or university, and perhaps for the first part of your career, consider where emphasis was placed:

- the acquisition of knowledge;
- the testing of knowledge;
- completing work accurately and quickly.

In other words, the emphasis was always on the first two dimensions! To develop successfully in your career, a new emphasis must be placed on developing the dimension of trust. You can do this with your friends, your family, and your workmates. The tool to use: networking.

Networking Redux

As we have previously reviewed, relationship-building skills – and therefore your network – are critical for business development. And business development skills are a key consideration for promotion eligibility. It therefore follows that to be considered for promotion in many organizations, you need to have strong networking skills. If you are looking for a promotion, and you haven't mastered networking skills *as we've defined them,* a promotion may be further away than you think. More reason to become a master networker: this key skill will determine your success no matter what your career goal may be.

FOCUS

- The Price/Expertise/Trust model can be used whether you are selling your organization's services or selling yourself.

ACTION CHECKLIST

❑ Be a giver, not a taker: if you haven't started the Give to Get process yet, look for at least one person that you can start with today.

Chapter 23:
Adjusting to Change

CHAPTER IN A FLASH: *Your likelihood of success after a change is often predicated on what you do beforehand. Understanding the differences between your current role and the new one can lead to a strategy to surmount any gap.*

Define Yourself Broadly

Earlier in this book we discussed briefly the problems that can ensue if you have always defined yourself solely in terms of your job. After you have achieved your goal, the problem will no longer be theoretical: it's real. It is a challenge to describe yourself in a new role, division, or level comfortably, especially when you've just made the switch. Here are some suggestions that might make it easier:

1. Strive to describe yourself in non-job terms when outside the workplace. Diversifying yourself to be "more than your job" is critical to achieving balance. Remember the Mikey story: "I'm in finance, but my real interests are in the area of…"

2. When asked directly about your new job, position, or enterprise, answer with a crisp, prepared, memorized response. While it may sound contrived at first, you will quickly develop comfort with the new words.

Dress for Success

How you look makes a big impression on those around you. Especially when you meet someone for the first time, your shoes, clothing, and personal grooming will peg you into a certain category. We touched on this earlier, but in the context of Personal Branding.

As a consultant, the rule has always been to dress just slightly more formally than the client. If you are dressed too casually, you lose credibility. If you are dressed too formally, you appear arrogant. While this rule of thumb seems simple, my team ran into an interesting situation with one client. The senior executives all wore suits and ties, but everyone else in the organization wore casual business attire. What to do if you're meeting both in the same day? In this case, we decided we would wear dark blue blazers and white shirts, with an open collar and no tie. When we were with the middle managers, we took off our blazers; when we were with the executives, the jackets stayed on.

Why bother paying such close attention to your clothing? Because it is hard enough selling your ideas to others. Paying attention to how you are perceived makes selling your ideas to your colleagues or clients just that much easier.

How different is your new position from your old one? Look in your closet, and make sure that your wardrobe is appropriate given both your new position and the culture of your new workplace. Several years ago, I found myself promoted from one role to another. One of my staff members was kind enough to point out to me that my clothes must match my new role, not my old one. A bit embarrassing, but very, very helpful.

You only have one chance to make a good first impression.

Home Offices

There is always the story of those who work from home, who amble from bedroom to office, wearing only a bathrobe or lounging clothes. To keep some degree of separation between your home mindset and your work mindset, always dress in appropriate office attire. You'll feel different if you dress for success, whether you're with people at a meeting or on the phone in your office. Postscript: you can dress for success and dress for comfort at the same time. If your wardrobe doesn't allow it, go shopping for a wardrobe that does.

Quickly Reset Your Expectations

If you have moved to a different division, functional area, office, or employer, remember that your expectations have been well-conditioned to The Way It Is Done. Think about the changes. Are admin policies always tightly enforced or is there flexibility? Which is more highly valued: getting in early or staying late? What is the role of a staff department, such as HR, compared to the line manager? How much power is there at the head office compared to those out in the field?

If you are going to make any type of change, these questions and many others should not be taken for granted. It is better to leave your expectations at the door and approach your new role with an open attitude of learning. Remember, some of your previous success was due to your previous organizational knowledge. Doesn't it make sense to invest time developing knowledge in your "new" surroundings, before enforcing your assumptions on it? Doing this helps you reset your expectations and will ultimately reduce your personal frustrations as you adjust.

Gap Analysis

The "gap" theory in quality management is this: whenever there is a mismatch between expectations and what actually happens, a gap is created. This gap is translated into client disappointment, which then translates to bad word-of-mouth and lost repeat sales. If expectations are consistently exceeded, the reverse happens: clients are delighted, they come back for more, and they refer their friends.

What are the key differences between your old role and your new one?

The differences between your old and new roles may also expose some gaps. Whether you're moving from a large organization to a small one, from the private sector to the public sector, or from a corporate position back into a professional services firm, the lay of the land will be different.

To help you, go through the following gap analysis. Using the chart below, list all the differences between your "old" and your "new" roles, across each of the dimensions shown. Then for each of these differences, write down coping strategies and action items. Do this several days before you start, and then revise it several days after you have arrived. Awareness of the differences is the first step to dealing with them properly.

An example coping strategy: if you have changed industries, a coping strategy might be to immerse yourself in knowledge about your new industry. Action items might include going to the library and getting several years' copies of the industry trade journals, soliciting your new colleagues' recommendations on the best books to read on the industry, and attending the annual trade conference. Financial analyst reports on the industry, company, and competitors can be helpful too.

Gap Analysis Chart

Dimension	Old Role	New Role	Coping Strategy	Action Items
Industry				
Organization size				
Organization structure				
Technology				
Processes – management				
Processes – accounting				
Processes – sales/marketing				
Processes – HR				
Processes – operations				
Job responsibilities				
Expectations of me				
External contact				
Workgroup size				
Resolving staff issues				
Relationships with staff				
Relationships with manager				

Expectations of Family and Friends

It is not just your own expectations that need some readjustment. In your prior role, you may have left for the office early each morning and returned at a certain time each evening. By definition, you were *at* work, earning a living. If your new position demands travel, it is import to advise those around you as to what the "new normal" is. (It is also important to ensure that quality time with family and friends is not reduced, just moved around a bit.)

If your new position is one that has you working from a home office or with non-standard hours, you may find families and friends assuming that you are not working. Since you no longer go *to* work, they may assume that you no longer *do* work. You may find yourself deluged with requests to do home-based chores, pick up the kids, arrange for a service call, do the laundry, or any other number of non-work activities. Of course, you can choose to do as much of this as you wish. This speaks once again to the importance of setting expectations properly: even though you might not be doing the same thing as before, you are most definitely working, and there are some boundaries that you can't cross.

A personal anecdote can illustrate this. We had just moved into a new house in a wonderful community. One of the features of the house was an oversized study on the main floor. My wife and I decided to share the study, so we could share computer peripherals and both have ready access to personal files. This worked out very well until my job changed and I had to maintain a home office. At that point, it still worked out very well... during the day when no one was around. When my wife came home and decided to check her email in her half of the study, I found it completely impossible to concentrate on phone meetings or my own important work. For some reason, I always felt that she was looking over my shoulder, which of course was not the case! How would you solve this problem? If the door to the study is closed, I am still at work, engaged in a phone meeting where I am not to be disturbed under any circumstance. Expectations set – expectations met.

Reset the expectations of family and friends. They are used to the "old you".

A former colleague experienced this problem in a different way. She was in her mid-50s and had left the corporate world to become a free agent. She was busier than ever, consulting to a host of credible clients. Whenever she saw her friends, all of whom were still in the corporate world, she would be asked how retirement was going. This type of irritating comment, which implied that she was old and had little value left to give, took a while to eradicate.

Expectations also need to be set regarding your new compensation. Perhaps your new plan has bonuses distributed differently. Perhaps you are an entrepreneur, and you are in the "lean" start-up phase. If you are used to automatic deposits of a standard pay amount, getting used to a "lumpy" compensation plan may mean that you must also change *when* you spend your money.

Financial Success and mid-Course Corrections

How much do you intend to make, and when? If you have a corporate position, are you on track to making your bonus? If you are an entrepreneur, how closely are you tracking to your budget? Letting those around you understand your objectives will help you to achieve them. If something isn't working exactly as you had originally planned, remember the importance of making mid-course corrections. And if the grass isn't as green as you thought it might be, don't discount the possibility of returning to your previous employer: after all, that's where you had your initial career success.

If you haven't burned any bridges, you may find there to be a surprising amount of interest. Another wise idea: make sure that your business partners and any family are up to speed as you make these changes. They have as much at stake in your success as you do.

Maintain and Rely on Your Network

Just because you are in a new role doesn't mean that your "old" network no longer has any value. While there are only so many hours during the day, time must be found to keep the network ticking. This doesn't mean the continuous knocking on doors looking for sales. And it doesn't mean a Christmas card each year. It means that each member of your network is on a specific Give to Get contact cycle. Review Chapter 17 for the mechanics of doing this efficiently.

About the only time you might be excused for sending out a "broadcast" form letter to all your contacts is when you start a new role. It is the one time that you can brag, without appearing to be a braggart. Take the time to do it, hopefully within the first month of your start. On each letter, pen a short personal note to the recipient – they'll appreciate it.

Give to Get is a critical and ongoing career development activity.

Slowly Repair Your Damaged Bridges

Despite your best efforts, whenever there is a change, people are sometimes hurt, and they become upset with you. They may feel hard done by because of some tough decisions you made during your tenure. They may hold a grudge over a simple misunderstanding. Or maybe they hold you responsible for their being passed over for promotion. Because you are no longer there, you might not even be aware of their animus.

Although time does heal wounds, grudges tend to fester and get worse with age. It takes very little effort to nurture damaged relationships back to health, and the time is well worth it. Particularly if you once worked well together, it may be that you can work together again sometime in the future. If you don't think you will ever work with that individual, in any type of relationship, be practical: a terribly negative relationship will poison your reputation for years. Give to Get is the primary mechanism to reach out and start the repair work. Over time, people will remember more of the value that you are giving than past history. Repair the bridge!

Focus

Every minute of the day has value, and unfortunately, each minute wasted is gone forever. For this reason more than anything else, each task you set yourself must be focused on driving your agenda forward. Busywork, procrastination, and half-efforts are your worst enemies.

Most people, especially successful ones, usually assume they have focus already. But that doesn't mean improvement is impossible. Here are a few suggestions:

- Review your job objectives or your business plan a few weeks after any change. Ask yourself how many of your current daily or weekly activities directly move you closer to achieving your goals.

Avoid being distracted by activities that lead you away from your goals.

- Write your objectives on a whiteboard or poster, mounted conspicuously in your office. Not only will the posting remind you of your goals, it will remind others too.

- Which of your regular meetings are not productive, and why? Fix this problem before even more of your time is drained away.

- How much time is spent on political issues and what-might-be guessing, instead of driving to your goals? Politics and gossip can become a huge distraction if left to run their course: stop them in their tracks.

- Which of your colleagues drain your time, either with mindless questions or because you have to fix their mistakes? In both cases, you have been taken away from your focus. Unfortunately, in both cases, your colleague doesn't have focus either.

- Review exactly how you spent your time the previous day. Where were the wasted minutes, and how can you avoid the wastage in the future?

- Finally, remember that you are working for a reason. Review your Personal Balance Sheet again, and make sure that the balance you now have is the balance you want.

Remember Your Strengths

Even though much might have changed in your day-to-day life since you've taken on your new role, you are still the same person. It is very easy to lose confidence and begin harboring self-doubts. The first three months after a change are especially challenging; give yourself time, and don't beat yourself up because of an occasional blip. It is easy for others to criticize from the sidelines, especially since they don't walk in your shoes each day. Disregard the naysayers and focus on your goals. Remember, there is no investment return without some degree of risk.

If you find it all a bit overwhelming, go back to those who have traditionally given you emotional and professional support, and ask for more. It is absolutely reasonable to tell them your concerns, and ask for their advice. Among those on your Reality Check Interview list, your mentors, your family, and your friends, there are plenty of folks who want to see you succeed. Giving them a chance to help you is important for you and very flattering for them.

After leaving a difficult organization, some people are so low that they have no confidence left to lose. One public-sector manager who left under these circumstances described the situation succinctly: "When I left, I *knew* that I could do nothing. When I got my first independent contract, I couldn't believe it – I thought it was luck." If this is partly the case in your situation, look again at the exercise in self-labeling in Chapter 11. And remember that what underlies your past success will drive your future success too.

Remember Your First Few Jobs

Remember your first full-time position? While you probably now recognize how green you were back then, see beyond that inexperience and recall what you did that helped you achieve your success. Although some people chalk it up to their luck, intelligence, or drive, most people will admit that their attitude had a lot to do with it.

What was *your* attitude back then? As a new hire, you were allowed to be naive, asking dumb questions. You were expected to be keen. And it sure was appreciated when you rolled up your sleeves without complaint and attacked a problem with the rest of the team. Fast-forward to today. Why can't you use these same attitudes in your new position?

ASK THE DUMB QUESTIONS: People will appreciate that you value their expertise.

BE KEEN: They will see your enthusiasm for the job, and it will be infectious.

ROLL UP YOUR SLEEVES: Your colleagues will see that you're one of the team – not an arrogant new hire from outside.

DON'T BE AFRAID OF MAKING MISTAKES: If you always play it safe, you'll never win the race. When an inevitable mistake occurs, take responsibility for it, learn from it, and then move on.

Isolation

In your previous role, you had a built-in, automated social network. People you didn't know so well greeted you warmly and exchanged pleasantries. Tight bonds of trust formed while working long hours on important projects. You developed real friendships with many people, socializing both after working hours and while traveling on business.

Isolation gives you a chance to focus, at precisely the time you need it most.

In your new role, the workplace social-support network may need to be developed anew. If you follow an entrepreneurial path, your social network might not even include a single employee. If you are working from home, you must deal with both isolation and separation.

Isolation can be a real shock, but it can also be a real opportunity, as there is no hiding from it. You are forced to develop your workplace social network. The new people you meet will be different and refreshing from what you're used to. Isolation also provides you an opportunity to focus, at precisely the time you need it most.

Those who feel the isolation most acutely (often entrepreneurs or caregivers) can do several practical things to lessen the impact:

- Schedule a minimum of three out-of-the-office meetings per week, with networking peers, suppliers, and prospects.

- If some of the work can be done at clients' or suppliers' premises, consider doing the work there, rather than at a home office.

- Use technology to help. Before, you may have walked around the office to catch up with people, but now you must do so electronically. Get used to using the telephone, email, and especially instant messaging to stay in contact with your clients, suppliers, and partners. Just remember, though, that electronic communication etiquette is a bit different than traditional communication etiquette. Nobody appreciates being interrupted by short emails that say "How's it going," no matter how friendly the intent.

- Review your after-hours activities, and slant them toward ones that give you the social interaction you are looking for. If you belong to a fitness club, for example, don't use the stationary bicycle by yourself – sign up for a group spinning class instead.

For those in new corporate or institutional positions, isolation is far easier to address. It can be as simple as sitting with different colleagues each day at lunch, to better understand their role in the organization.

Several years ago, my company appointed a new divisional president. As an outsider, he didn't really know anyone. One of his first objectives was to meet, either on the phone or in person, everyone in the organization. He set up visits to client sites and scheduled phone calls, meetings, breakfasts, lunches, and dinners. It took him about three months to do the rounds, but by then, he really understood the challenges and opportunities the company faced.

Avoid isolation by reaching out to those around you.

What did he talk about to those he met? He asked about their jobs, competitors, customers, challenges, and priorities. At the same time, he started the process of developing personal relationships.

Where Did My Mentors Go?

The issue of your changed relationships with your mentors is coupled partly with the issue of isolation. As discussed earlier, after a change (and especially if you leave the organization), your internal mentors may feel that you are ungrateful. They may feel snubbed. Or they may feel that their role is to mentor people only for the good of the team: with you gone, you no longer qualify for their time.

Nevertheless, if you feel there is benefit from the relationship, you should pursue an open, honest discussion with them on the subject. Recall how it was their mentoring over the years that developed your insight... which eventually led to your decision to make a change. Let them know that you still value their insight and acumen and would like to maintain the relationship for mutual benefit. Listen to what they have to say. Finally, don't forget to include them in your schedule for follow-up.

That being said, you may wish to change who you consider to be on your mentorship "A-List." You are in a new position – perhaps a new department, industry, role, company size, or location. If you could start from scratch, given your new reality, whom would you want as a mentor?

Starting a mentorship is straightforward, if you remember that it is a slow, mutual, step-by-step process. Ask your potential mentor for advice one day. Then ask them again some time later. Then ask them again some time after that. If the personal relationship develops at the same time as the professional one, you are on your way. Above all remember Give to Get: the mentor needs to get something out of the relationship too. What are you doing to give back? And what did you give them *before your first ask*? Mentoring relationships are like any other: if it is always a one-way street, it won't last. Finally, remember that not everyone is cut out to be a mentor and not all who are capable are willing.

If you don't use your mentors, you lose them. Years ago, I developed a great relationship with my barber, Luigi. He was of the old school and always had some wisdom from his childhood that he was keen to pass on. For several years I hadn't seen him, as I had grown my hair and clearly didn't need a barber. When I returned to my usual monthly haircut, I asked for him at his shop and was greeted by the sad faces of his colleagues. Luigi had died six months earlier, of a stroke. He was in his early 60s. Sometimes you lose your mentors through no fault of your own, and when they are gone, their wisdom goes with them.

Reset Your Infrastructure

Your past success has been helped by the infrastructure around you. Sometimes this infrastructure is a technology department that quickly solves your problem, an assistant who handles your travel arrangements, or a graphic designer who makes your presentations beautiful. Other times the infrastructure is in the enterprise software that seemingly automates much of the bookkeeping.

In your new role, these services may be delivered differently, or perhaps not at all. You might be expected to personally do things that were done by others in your previous position, or vice versa. Get used to asking questions that start with "Typically, how does one..." or "What is the fastest way to..."

If you are on your own or in a very small business, consider outsourcing as much as possible of the infrastructure to specialists.

- Hire a bookkeeper instead of maintaining the accounting system yourself.
- Develop a good relationship with a full-service travel agency.

- Scout out a full-service print shop that can also do some basic graphic design.

- Ask some of your "independent" friends whom they use to help solve their computer problems. There are plenty of clever, helpful technical folks out there: the problem is finding them.

- Professional recruiters may also be able to assist you with certain HR issues, or at least point you in the right direction. If you are just looking for resumés, an on-line job board may be all you need.

- Insurance agents can help determine what additional coverage you may require and can often function as your entire pensions and benefits infrastructure.

Unearned Authority

Differences can add up, whether it be in your title, role, industry, company size, or some other dimension. In your new role, don't make the assumption that you have the same power and authority as in your last one. After all, presumably much of your past authority was earned by you one step at a time. Your new authority, if you are in a corporate role, comes with your title, *but is not yet earned.* Until you have earned it, expect a different dynamic when dealing with your colleagues.

> Despite a fancy new title, you will only have real authority after you've earned it.

Differences beyond your personal position also have an impact, especially when dealing with external groups. If you have moved from a larger to a smaller organization, your supplier contacts (and the services you received) were likely geared to the buying power of that larger company. While they would likely be polite to you if you contacted them for help, you might find yourself shunted to distributors who work only with smaller accounts such as yours. The reverse is also very true. Review the Gap Analysis Chart earlier in this chapter, and take a closer look at your Coping Strategies and Action Items. Are they still relevant, or do they need some finesse?

For many people going through the career planning process, there will be no major change, for the simple reason that they are very happy in their current role. Others will not make a change because they are busy filling in the gaps. Nevertheless, each of these concepts (attitude, isolation, mentors, infrastructure, and authority) may also partly apply to you.

FOCUS

- Define yourself broadly by describing yourself along many dimensions.

- Dress for success.

- Reset your expectations, and while you're at it, reset those of your friends and family.

- Remember that your professional relationships can last a lifetime. Slowly repair your damaged bridges and continue to build on the relationships that you currently have.

- Have confidence in yourself: those who hired you do. (And so do your friends, family, and mentors.)

- Remember what it was like to start your first job. Rekindle that keen attitude!

- Earn your authority.

ACTION CHECKLIST

❑ Complete the Gap Analysis chart.

Chapter 24:
Using an Extended Leave

CHAPTER IN A FLASH: *An extended leave can recharge you, but only if you structure your time and set goals. At the end of the leave you will want to look back and consider your time well-spent.*

Most people who "get rich quick" enjoy what they're doing and usually get rich as a by-product of the passion they have for what they do. Those who strive only for the goal and not the journey are missing the point. The journey should be just as exciting, if not more so, than the destination.

What is a sabbatical? It can be either a short break (two to three months) or one that is longer, often up to a year. It is a time that can be used to disconnect from your normal work patterns and reconnect to your priorities. Some organizations have sabbatical programs, but a sabbatical is often taken between jobs, or perhaps as an unpaid leave from a long-term employer. Needless to say, the more senior you are, the tougher it is for the employer to fill your shoes while you are away, and therefore the less likely that they would allow you to leave for an extended period.

> An extended leave is a chance for you to recharge, achieve short-term goals, or test-drive a major change.

Many people spend hours considering their retirement plans. They dream of golfing all day. Then sitting on a charitable board in the evening. Spending months each year traveling. At the same time, they'll learn to play the piano, write a book, and spend more time with family and friends.

There is a good chance, however, that you will be disappointed with some of the realities of retirement. What if you can't do it all? Arthritis plagues your fingers, so learning the piano is out. Fatigue may limit your evening activities. And unfortunately, your significant other has long developed his or her own interests, separate from yours, because of all the time you spent at work. Or even worse, you (or your significant other) may succumb to ill health and not even make it to retirement. Taking an extended leave gives you the opportunity to do some of these "fun" things now, while you still have the inclination, energy, and health.

WHAT IS THE VALUE OF A BREAK? Consider: you can spend up to 40 years of your life working, and then have 20 years of retirement. Would three months (or one year) not be more valuable earlier in life than at retirement? Yes. But why then are sabbaticals not commonplace? People don't take sabbaticals for the same reason they don't quit their job. Financial commitments, desire to keep up with the Joneses, desire to maintain seniority, and perceived risk are but a few of the reasons to stay.

Probably the most important reason to take an extended break is if you are feeling the onset of burn-out. After investing so many years in your education, after earning certification after certification, and (hopefully) after a number of promotions, it would be a shame if you started hating the very thing you once loved. Taking a sabbatical will allow you to recharge, and then later recommit to your career. The same capability that gave you your success so far will be the capability that powers you on your return.

Three-Month Sabbatical

What should you do when you take three months of your retirement and spend it earlier on a sabbatical? Certain things come to mind: recharge, achieve short-term goals, reconnect with family and friends, and evaluate your career plan.

At the beginning of the sabbatical, you may feel disconnected from the hectic nature of your previous position. Your workplace social network will no longer exist. You will not have the deadlines and the demands of a day-to-day position. And you may find time starting to slip by faster than you think.

For all these reasons, it is critically important to set clear objectives for yourself, and set a firm weekly schedule. Here's a suggestion for setting your objectives: start with your Personal Balance Sheet (Chapter 6), and see what comes to mind. If there has always been a sport or hobby that you wanted to start (golf, tennis, music, etc.) but never had time to, consider doing so on your break.

In addition to any ideas generated by your Personal Balance Sheet, it will be important to set two additional objectives for yourself:

1. **Satisfy your need for a social network.** This might be as simple as going out for several networking lunches each week or getting involved in your community.

2. **Complete, by the end of the sabbatical, a revised Career Commitment Chart.** Re-read this book, and re-do the exercises within it. You will find that time off will give you a more focused perspective on your personal and professional goals.

Setting objectives for your sabbatical can help answer questions from your curious (and likely jealous) friends and colleagues. More importantly, it will give you a sense of purpose. At the end of your sabbatical, you will be able to look back and point to specific, achieved accomplishments.

One-Year Sabbatical

With a year break, you can try something very different, often with your family: travel abroad, study, etc. You can possibly complete a major life goal, such as completing an advanced degree or undertaking a physical challenge.

Set objectives and a schedule for yourself.

Because of the significant length of time that you are away from the workforce, it is even more important to set objectives and a schedule for yourself. Even if it seems too "business-like," spend a few minutes each month ensuring that you are on track to achieving your objectives. If you aren't, either change your activities or change your objectives.

Entrepreneurial friends of mine, after selling their company, decided that a one-year sabbatical would give them a fresh life experience. After considering several alternatives, they moved to Beijing. They attended university there as full-time students, learning Mandarin during the week and sightseeing each weekend. After their year was up, they went back to being entrepreneurs, starting a corporate research company, with headquarters in… Beijing.

Whether your sabbatical is three months long or twelve, at some point you will return to the workforce. While you may have a new appreciation for things you missed while working, you may also feel a sense of loss. Consider the objectives and activities you set for yourself while you were away. Maybe you had set goals relating to personal fitness and spending time with your family. Will the end of your sabbatical also mean spending less time with your family and gaining back all that weight? Hopefully not, but there are only so many hours in the day, and something has to give.

Before you return to work, update your Personal Balance Sheet.

Before you return to the working world, get out your Personal Balance Sheet and update it. Although you might not have time to do everything on your return, defining your priorities will help you achieve at least a modicum of balance. And also help keep that extra weight off.

Maternity or Parental Leave

Each jurisdiction has different laws regarding maternity or parental leave; your employer likely has policies that will affect you as well. If you will be taking time off to care for a new child, your priorities will be highly focused on your new responsibilities. But are there other personal or professional objectives you want to consider at the same time?

"I Can't Do It Because I Can't Afford It"

It is always easier to close doors than to think how to walk through them. From a financial standpoint, it seems that the "hit" taken from losing three months' salary is substantial. You might be thinking to yourself that it is tough to make ends meet as it is. But if it really is important to you, in 480 months of a typical career, can you not find three months to take a break?

From a purely practical standpoint, financing a sabbatical requires planning and forethought. Here are some ideas to consider:

- **Realistically estimate lower expenditure levels.** Plan to put yourself on a strict budget while away from the workforce, but test it out beforehand to see if you can live with it. Consider what you might be able to give up or replace with cheaper alternatives (expensive restaurant meals, for example).

- **If you have a mortgage, negotiate to reduce your payments.** This can be done by extending the amortization, reducing the rate, or both. Often, this is the biggest single expenditure that one has, and reducing payments for a few months can provide the highest relief. Make sure, though, that you can increase payments back to a higher amount once your leave is over.

- **Save your vacations.** In the period before your sabbatical, don't use any of your vacation – save it to help fund your time off. If you currently have four weeks' annual leave and you are able to get by without any vacation throughout this year at all, then *one-third of your three-month sabbatical is already paid for.* If you have a longer amount of accrued vacation, it looks even better. Depending on when you wish to take your sabbatical, your employer may allow you to borrow time from your next year's allotment – further reducing your financial burden.

- **Review your insurance plans.** Are there savings that can be generated by reviewing your life and disability insurance? Are there cheaper plans that offer the same level of coverage? And while you are away, what is the cost of medical, dental, and other health coverage?

There are often other hidden savings that we can access. Some insurance policies, for example, have a cash value that grows each month. Can your policy be collapsed and replaced with a policy that provides coverage but doesn't include a savings component? (Or failing that, can you "borrow" your own money from the plan, at a preferential interest rate?) Be careful about making changes to your insurance coverage without speaking to a qualified insurance professional and financial planner.

• **Raid your savings.** Although this doesn't sound exactly appealing to most people, it is truly a matter of perspective. If you consider your sabbatical as part of your retirement, but taken earlier, where is the harm in spending some of your retirement savings earlier as well? Of course, the financially minded will point out that any money taken from retirement savings is money that cannot grow over time. And of course, they'd be right. If you decide to raid your retirement savings, you should consider all the consequences and govern yourself accordingly. If you have a rainy day fund, a sabbatical would certainly qualify as a worthwhile place to use it.

• **Review your employer's policies.** Some employers have specific policies regarding sabbaticals. You may find that certain benefits remain covered while away. Or that you are eligible for a paid leave after a certain number of years. Or that they are only permitted during certain times of the year. Knowledge of your organization's policies (if they have them) will make it easier to talk to your manager about the possibility of an extended leave.

International Transfers

The decision to pull up all your roots and move to another part of the world is both a scary and an exciting prospect. Although a full discussion of this type of move is beyond the scope of this book, much of the thinking you did and goals you set (within the Personal Balance Sheet, for example) can set the context to ascertain whether a permanent move makes sense.

> International experience can give you greater perspective and depth.

Purely from a career standpoint, taking an international assignment can give greater depth to your knowledge and may be a necessary step for your advancement.

If you are looking to move first, then hope to find your next position when you are on the ground, don't deceive yourself. It is not easy. Consider that the cultural norms and business practices may be very different from what you're used to at home. Your personal network is more geographically bound to where you are now. Even your professional credentials may not be recognized in the new location. If you are working at an organization with international affiliations, use your internal connections to arrange a transfer abroad.

Priorities and Life Goals

If I were to die tomorrow, what is the one thing I'd be sorry I hadn't done? And if I were to die next week, next month, or next year?

These questions help quickly prioritize what we might want to do next. For tomorrow, the answer might be to tell your spouse or children that you loved them. Next week? Maybe you always wanted to see a part of the world, and there's just enough time to do it. If you knew you were to die next month, maybe you would want to use the time to develop better relationships with your friends and family. Maybe work on a personal legacy project.

How many of these priorities are reflected in your Personal Balance Sheet? (They should be.)

What to do if you were to die next year is a little tougher, but only because the possibilities widen greatly. This is why thinking about the long-term tomorrow is so connected with your Personal Balance Sheet, and how we use each and every day. "Today" is your opportunity to start doing what matters.

When I'm retired and look back, what will I see?

Will you be satisfied with what you've accomplished, or will you wonder how you wasted so much time on unimportant matters? Will you be satisfied with a tombstone that says "Always met his deadlines"?

Consider once again your Personal Balance Sheet. At the end of your life, would you not want it to read "Mission Accomplished"? If so, then the only thing that separates you from achievement is time, and how you use it. Your Personal Balance Sheet and Career Commitment Chart give this to you.

Career Maturity

Our career really started eariler when we were in school. As we attended each class, we discovered what we enjoyed and what we were good at.

The subjects we took, at least at the beginning, were mandated. That was appropriate, as we didn't yet have the maturity, nor the life experience, to advocate for greater choice. The higher up the educational ladder we went, the more opportunity for choice (and specialization) became available to us.

When we got our first job, we continued learning, and as we mastered each skill, we were rewarded with one promotion after another. Some of these jobs were enjoyable, while others we viewed only as stepping stones for something even better.

Today, we are compressing so much experience considerably earlier in our careers: many feel that a mid-life crisis has hit far earlier than in previous generations. The first part of the Personal Balance Sheet provides many reasons for this, but one reason stands out. With more experience, you have developed the maturity to know what you want in life and in your career. The SkillChecks, Job Quality Checklist, Personal Balance Sheet, Career Commitment Chart, Reality Check Interviews, and other tools helped crystallize your thoughts and presented them in a way that translates knowledge into action.

You feel empowered. You are no longer willing to delegate your career progress to others. And you recognize that work-life balance is your responsibility – not someone else's. Your success to date has proven you have the strength of mind to achieve any goal you set for yourself.

FOCUS

- Sabbaticals can be useful time-outs to recharge your energy and reconnect with family or friends. If you decide to take one, make sure that you set clear objectives for yourself. Objectives provide structure to your time and when achieved, leave you with confidence and pride.

- Your career should help you achieve your life goals. Use every minute of every day productively, for once time passes, it can't be recaptured.

- By going through the exercises in this book every two years (or whenever there is a major change in your life), you will have the tools to master your destiny, on the job and in your life.

ACTION CHECKLIST

❑ Review and revise your action items and target dates, paying particular attention to those items that you can start (or complete) sooner.

Chapter 25:
Your Ten Next Steps

CHAPTER IN A FLASH: *While your next steps might not be in the same order as the ones in this chapter, unless you translate what you've learned into action, you will achieve neither your professional nor your personal goals.*

1. Fill out the Personal Balance Sheet, and act on it. Don't let "too much work" be an excuse for "not enough life."

2. Clarify your strengths, and learn from others: Reality Check Interviews.

3. An investment in yourself always pays off: sign up for a course on anything, immediately. Once your career plan is firmed up, you can be pickier, but meanwhile, get back in the mode of learning.

4. Network: Attend one association or professional group meeting per month; meet new people in an area of personal or professional interest. And remember Give to Get: find ways to help others win, and they will return the favor.

5. Without a plan, you won't know where you're going: fill out the Career Commitment Chart.

6. Engage your manager and HR processes. You'll need their support to succeed, so begin the process of discussion. Part of this is to make sure that appropriate action items from your Personal Balance Sheet and Career Commitment Chart are embedded into your organization's employee evaluation and planning paperwork.

7. Once you know your goals, professional and personal, clear away the activities that don't move you closer to them.

8. Calendarize the action plans from your Career Commitment Chart, and commit to doing one thing before the week is out.

9. Reinforce the concepts: Sign up for the *Make It Happen Tipsheet* at www.PersonalBalanceSheet.com.

10. Set your BlackBerry to turn off at night. Take advantage of your day of rest. And get a good sleep each night. Create the time to live a balanced life.

THE MOST IMPORTANT POINT IN THIS BOOK:

*Career planning is an activity that
requires no one's permission to do,
and whose beneficiary is primarily you.*

THE SECOND MOST IMPORTANT POINT IN THIS BOOK:

*A plan is great, but unless it actually gets implemented,
it has limited value. Calendarize at least a few of the
Ten Next Steps, and commit to start this week.*

Afterword

During the first several years of your career, you gain experience, develop new skills, and eventually get promoted to more senior responsibilities. As you mature in your career, you develop perspective and a nascent understanding of your real priorities.

Nevertheless, many people float from opportunity to opportunity as each is presented: they continue to learn, continue to develop new skills, and continue to get promoted. At some point they recognize that their work-life balance is not where they want it to be. And they realize that their career direction isn't where they want it to be either.

Since no one knows you better than yourself, there is no one better equipped than you to determine your goals and how to achieve them. Delegating this task to your employer, your friends, or your mom will result in you chasing their dreams, not your own.

If you diligently go through this book, the equation changes profoundly. You learn the tools and the vocabulary to define, and then control your priorities. You learn how to engage your many supporters: family, friends, colleagues, and managers. You learn that managing your career is a process that requires an investment in time. And finally, you learn that with that investment comes an important return: a more fulfilling career and stronger personal relationships. Perhaps Winston Churchill said it best: "We make a living by what we get, but we make a life by what we give."

Appendices

Appendix 1: Frameworks

❑ **SKILLCHECK I (CHAPTER 5):** Helps you pull together a listing of areas where you may have had great interest or where you have developed special skills.

1. What is your educational and training background? (Include university, professional certifications, internal and external seminars)

2. Look back at your college or university transcripts. Was there a course that you found interesting, but you never did follow up or take more advanced training? Why was it interesting?

3. What specific skills did you hone to excellence in your previous three roles (or serving your last three clients)?

4. What aspects of your previous three roles provided the greatest satisfaction?

5. What areas of knowledge or skill do you see as your biggest weakness?

6. What non-work activities provide you the most satisfaction? What is it about these activities that interest you?

7. Which sections of the newspaper do you read first? Which magazines and online newsletters do you subscribe to?

☐ **SKILLCHECK II (CHAPTER 5):** An inventory to help assess your comfort level with different expertise types, and areas that may require upgrading.

Self Assessment: Basic/Intermediate/Guru	General Management and Miscellaneous
_____	Turnarounds and Restructuring
_____	Process Re-engineering
_____	Project Management
_____	Internal Consultant
_____	Business Unit Head
_____	Focus Group Facilitation
_____	Board-level Experience
_____	Corporate Secretary
_____	Legal Experience – Transactions
_____	Legal Experience – Advocacy
_____	Legal Experience – Policy
_____	Strategic Planning
_____	Sustainability
_____	Research and Development
_____	International Management _____
_____	Professional Certifications _____
_____	Other _____
	Sales
_____	Sales Management
_____	Sales Forecasting
_____	Sales (deals <100K)
_____	Sales (deals between 100K and 1M)
_____	Sales (deals >1M)
_____	Pre-sales Support
_____	Other _____
	Finance and Accounting
_____	CFO
_____	Regulatory Compliance
_____	Corporate Finance – Banks and Other Lenders
_____	Corporate Finance – Public Markets/Regulatory Issues
_____	Investor Relations/Creditor Relations
_____	Audit – Public Companies
_____	Audit – Small and Medium-Sized Enterprises
_____	Internal Audit
_____	Treasury, Cash Management, Foreign Exchange
_____	Budgeting
_____	Performance measurement
_____	Controller, Accounting, Statement Preparation/Review
_____	Bookkeeping

_____	Management Accounting (including Activity-Based Costing)
_____	Valuations
_____	Financial Analysis
_____	Mergers, Acquisitions, and Divestitures
_____	Receivership and Insolvency
_____	Risk Management
_____	Forensic Accounting and Investigations
_____	Real Estate
_____	International Tax
_____	Corporate Tax
_____	Commodity Tax
_____	Personal Tax
_____	Financial Planning
_____	Financial Management Software (_____)
_____	Tax Software (_____)
_____	Other _____

MIS

_____	Senior IT Management (e.g., CIO or similar)
_____	Computer Audit
_____	IT Program Management
_____	Technical Architecture
_____	Programming, Network, and System-Related Functions
_____	Change Management
_____	Business Analyst
_____	Technical Writer
_____	Implementation of an ERP System
_____	Implementation of a CRM System
_____	Implementation of a Successful e-Commerce System
_____	Other _____

Marketing

_____	Advertising
_____	Market Research
_____	Product Development
_____	Brand Strategy
_____	Services Marketing
_____	Direct Marketing
_____	Internet Marketing
_____	Channel Management
_____	Corporate Identity
_____	CRM Software
_____	Media Relations/Public Relations
_____	Government Relations
_____	International Marketing
_____	Database Marketing
_____	Other _____

	Manufacturing, Production, and Supply Chain
_____	Factory Management
_____	Quality Systems and Management
_____	ERP Software (_____)
_____	Logistics/Transportation
_____	Import/Export
_____	Purchasing
_____	Inventory Management
_____	Data Management
_____	Other _____
	Human Resources
_____	Most Senior HR Manager
_____	HRIS Systems
_____	Payroll Systems
_____	Benefit and Pension Plans
_____	Compensation
_____	Recruitment
_____	HR Generalist
_____	Corporate Trainer
_____	Coaching/Mentoring
_____	Labor Negotiations
_____	Other _____
	Industry Vertical
_____	Retail
_____	Wholesale/Distributor
_____	Manufacturing
_____	Resource Sector
_____	Financial Services
_____	Professional Services
_____	Information Technology
_____	Telecom and Utilities
_____	Government/Public Services
_____	Non-Government/Non-profit Organizations
_____	Other _____

❏ **REALITY CHECK INTERVIEWS (CHAPTER 5):** Learn from the experience of others: what worked for them, and what didn't. At the same time, develop a new vocabulary to describe your strengths. List the names of the 30 people that you will interview:

1.	11.	21.
2.	12.	22.
3.	13.	23.
4.	14.	24.
5.	15.	25.
6.	16.	26.
7.	17.	27.
8.	18.	28.
9.	19.	29.
10.	20.	30.

❏ **PERSONAL BALANCE SHEET (CHAPTER 6):** A framework to help you plan a balance that is right for you, along with the action plan that will help you achieve it.

Dimension of Success	Goal at start of career	Goal five years ago	Current status (answers to questions)	Your next "goal"	◆
Community					
Family					
Intellectual					
Spiritual					
Physical					
Financial					
Career					

❏ **JOB QUALITY CHECKLIST (CHAPTER 9):** Consider whether it is time to contemplate a change to your job.

1. Are you still having fun?

2. Are you being challenged intellectually?

3. Do you like your colleagues?

4. Are you reaching your career goals?

5. Are you achieving life balance?

6. Is your compensation somewhat close to your worth?

❏ **TRIGGERING EVENTS LIST (CHAPTER 11):** A listing of possible events that might trigger a change.

1.
2.
3.
4.
5.

❏ **JOB QUALITY CHECKLIST REVIEW (CHAPTER 12):** A comparison of a potential position against the Job Quality Checklist criteria.

❏ **SELF-LABELING WORKSHEET (CHAPTER 14):** A framework to help you identify and remove labels that limit your performance.

Negative Labels

Label	First event	Refuted event (or plan)

Positive Labels

Label	First event

❑ **CAREER COMMITMENT CHART (CHAPTER 15):** A listing of your goals, along with the action plan required to achieve them.

	Career Goal	Action Items	Status/Milestone
Short term (within the year)			
Medium term (next few years)			
Longer term (5+ Years)			

❏ **NETWORKING NAME LIST (CHAPTER 17):** This categorizes all the people you know by the strength of their relationship to you. This is the raw material for your Give to Get process.

❏ **BUSINESS PLAN (CHAPTER 18):** This outlines each section of a basic business plan, for those considering starting their own business.

Executive Summary:
Business Description and Strategy:
Financial:
Marketing:
Sales:
Operations:
HR:

❏ **ELEVATOR PITCH (CHAPTER 20):** A 30-second answer to the question "what do you do?" Must be relevant to the listener.

❏ **GAP ANALYSIS CHART (CHAPTER 23):** Contrasts the differences between your current position and a future one, along with an action plan to bridge any gaps.

Dimension	Old Role	New Role	Coping Strategy	Action Items
Industry				
Organization size				
Organization structure				
Technology				
Processes – management				
Processes – accounting				
Processes – sales/marketing				
Processes – HR				
Processes – operations				
Job responsibilities				
Expectations of me				
External contact				
Workgroup size				
Resolving staff issues				
Relationships with staff				
Relationships with manager				

Appendix 2: Home Office Equipment List

- Computer (preferably a laptop).
- Software for office productivity, anti-virus, and back-up.
- Office-quality printer.
- High-speed Internet (e.g., cable or DSL broadband).
- Personal email address (don't forget to advise your family and long-time friends to send personal email here).
- Office-quality voicemail.
- Cell phone.
- Office supplies.
- Shredder.
- Private workplace (e.g., not the kitchen table).

Resources

Interested in more **Personal Balance Sheet** resources for yourself? Additional career development tips, resources, and online tools at www.PersonalBalanceSheet.com.

Looking for a Coach? Find out more about our coaching services at www.PersonalBalanceSheet.com, or contact Randall and his coaching team directly at request@PersonalBalanceSheet.com.

Looking for Career Development resources for your organization? Our Virtual Career Centre, accessible through www.PersonalBalanceSheet.com, empowers your employees to manage their careers, access special resources, and more.

Looking for a keynote or workshop that will motivate your group to action? Randall Craig's speaker site and contact information can be accessed at www.RandallCraig.com. Current topics include the following:

- **Achieve Life Balance:** With the increased pressure on employees to perform, the impact of *Work-Life Balance* programs are more important than ever. Unfortunately, most programs are designed from the perspective of the employee – how to get more life and less work – and are typically offered as part of a "wellness" package.

  This topic has three underlying goals: Retention, Productivity, and Motivation. Audience participants will be introduced to the *Personal Balance Sheet* by going through a number of reflective and interactive activities. Balance then becomes their personal responsibility – and not that of their employer. Each person will leave with a specific-to-them action plan, and a copy of a Personal Balance Sheet Action Planner.

- **Career Development:** Employee disengagement is one of the toughest management problems today. One of the root causes of this is a lack of control over personal destiny. Our Career Development seminar is designed to educate the employee about the subject, introduce the *Career Commitment Chart* planning tool, and then help them define a list of development activities that will help them achieve their self-selected goals.

✦ **Grow the Relationship to Make the Sale:** Whether you are selling a product, a service, or yourself, the relationship will always cement the deal. But how do you develop a relationship? Not everyone enjoys networking or schmoozing – so there must be another way. In this workshop, participants will be introduced to the *PET (Price/Expertise/Trust) Model* and learn a systematic way to develop and nurture relationships – and then how to close the sale. Participants will leave the workshop with a specific plan of action. NOTE: This workshop is delivered in three versions: for sales-oriented individuals (focus on business development), for existing employees (to improve teamwork), and for departing employees (for the job search).

✦ **MBA 101: Sharpening Your Business Acumen:** When was the last time your managers and staff were exposed to the newest ideas in management? How many of your great technical, sales, or administrative staff have been promoted but lack broader business skills? This intensive workshop fills in the gaps and goes over the key issues and concepts across the entire business enterprise. The first half of the session is devoted to learning the technical, from financial ratios, to supply chain, to viral marketing, and onwards; the second half is devoted to understanding behavior, using Herzberg, Maslow, and others. This session can be expanded into a half-day, full-day, or two-day workshop.

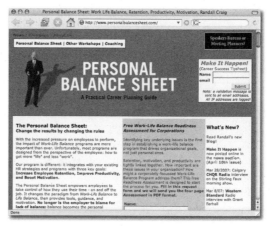

www.PersonalBalanceSheet.com